Watch and Pray

Portia Mange

ALL RIGHTS RESERVED. No part of this publication may be reproduced, stored in a retrieval system, or transmitted in any form or by any means – electronic, mechanical, photocopying, recording or otherwise – without written permission from the publisher, except per the provisions of the Copyright Act, 98 of 1978.

Unless otherwise identified: All scripture quotations, are taken from the New King James Version (NKJV) of the Holy Bible. Copyright © 1982 Thomas Nelson. Inc. Words meaning and definitions included are taken from Cambridge Dictionary and Wikipedia.

Copyright © 2019 Portia Mange
Watch and Pray
ISBN: 978-0-620-86856-3

Cover design: Stanley Maake
Published by: Nolo Publishers
Typeset in 12/13 Garamond by Stanley Maake
Printed by Nolo Publishers 1 2 3 4 5 1 2

≡NOLO
Publishers

Every effort has been made to obtain copyright permission for the material used in this book. Please contact the author with any queries in this regard.

DEDICATION

I would like to dedicate this book to Jehovah God, the Eternal Creator who inspires me by His Word and reveals Himself to me by His Spirit.

This book is also dedicated to my Family, specifically my husband and Priest Fortunate Mange, you are my source of courage, and my two sons, Blessing and Immanuel, as well as my beautiful daughter, Courage. You guys are my pillars of strength. Thank you for believing in me and loving me. To my mother and intercessor, Elizabeth Radingwane, Shalom.

To my departed Father, and my Prophet, Bishop Buyi Kumalo, Ms Millicent Kumalo and God's Kingdom Worship Centre Family (GKWC), you believed in me when I was in the lowest moments of my life. And you spoke the life changing word to me, and I will never forget. May God bless you and cause you to manifest in this generation. To Ackson and Faith Mwami, you are an inspiration to this generation, your inputs are appreciated. As you read this book you will experience the collision of miracles and breakthroughs this year and beyond.

El Bethel Family Church, you are a relevant Church of today, filled with God's presence. I love you.

This book is also dedicated to the entire church of Jesus Christ, and the Intercessors in South Africa and beyond. We press on in prayer and worship Elohim. Shalom!

Watch and Pray

ACKNOWLEDGEMENT

I would like to acknowledge Jesus Christ as my Lord and Saviour…

A Gift to: _____

From: _____

Notes

Name:
Contact Details:

Watch and Pray

ENDORSEMENTS!

Wow! This book has been packaged in truth and transparency which most believers can relate to. It is such a timely book for any believer.

In the perilous times that we live in, prayer is an essential key that authorizes the Lord to step and intervene into believers' affairs in accordance with what is written in their books of destinies.

Prayer is so critical that I believe it is the reason why it is mentioned 132 times in the Bible. Prayer is therefore an essential communication between God and man that gives Him the legal access into our lives. It is as important as breathing, and a believer's victory depends on how regular their communication with God is.

In James 4:3 it is clear that most believers do not live victorious lives that demonstrates the fulfilment of God's purpose in their lives. I believe lack of prayer and misplaced prayer is at the root of this. I believe, as believers read through the book, their prayer lives would improve and they will gain valuable insights from the wisdom Prophetess Portia shares in this book.

Mr Richard Anno-Frempong
Founder and Senior Pastor
Charismatic Christian Centre
Honeydew, South Africa

Watch and Pray

I count it a privilege and honour to pen an endorsement of this much needed relevant book of our time by this courageous prayer warrior. The book comes at a time where the world and body of Christ is hungry for answers. I have no doubt that it will enlighten and instil the importance of regular prayer. What is humbling about Ps Portia as a teacher of the Word and being highly anointed in the prophetic is the fact that, she relies on prayer as an integral part of her life and the power of the Holy Spirit by practically applying the principles of prayer through the Word of God. She is a living testimony of the power of prayer in her family, work environment and ministry.

I'm personally very proud of you together with the GKWC Family and I know my Husband would be equally proud, most of all, this is well pleasing to our Lord and Saviour.

And we continue to pray *"Lord show us your approval by making all our efforts successful" (Psalm 90:17).*

Morongwa Millicent Kumalo
God's Kingdom Worship Centre - Siyabuswa

I am excited to have witnessed the words of this book. Pastor Portia is a blessing and relevant prophetess of our time. This book will empower the readers, stir their faith to conspire and be in agreement with self, and conspire with God. Many times believers conspire and imagine against God through worry, doubt and unbelief. Prayer is the divine instrument that brings us to that dimension where nothing is impossible. This is a must read book and believers must conspire with God

Endorsements

against evil. We are called to conquer. God bless you as you watch and pray!

Bishop RW Mabasa
Forward in Faith Ministries

In this book, the Prophetess Portia brings a very unique element of prayer that is not only Word and Faith based but very prophetic.

This a kind of prayer that accurately predicts what will or must happen when bible believing believers pray against all odds. It is a result oriented prayer based on the relationship between God and his children, based upon the Word and the promises of God, who can't lie and with whom nothing is impossible.

The author is inspired to encourage and prepare the church for the great outpouring and the manifestation of the Supernatural works of God in these very last of the last days.

You can't read this book and remain the same.

Thank you very much. We pray that the message will reach and empower the body of Christ and challenge the unbelievers to follow God.

Stay blessed woman of the Most High God.

Bishop Sakhele M Makhubo
Endumisweni Covenant Church

Watch and Pray

I am encouraged by this book as it encourages intercessors, believers and those in the five-fold ministry to arise, pray and stand in the gap for individuals, churches and nations as watchmen. I believe this book is for all believers who are ready and willing to declare the will of God on earth on a consistent and regular basis. This is for believers who are not willing to stay by while the enemy plunders lives, homes, families and generations. This book is a manual that will encourage believers to engage in effective prayers. This book will empower you to override and overturn all evil predictions that are designed to destroy, manipulate or oppose the prophetic word over your live and enforce what is written concerning your life in the volume of your destiny books

Ms Maphefo Anno-Frempong
Associate Pastor
Charismatic Christian Centre, Honeydew, South Africa

CONTENTS

ENDORSEMENTS! .... a
FOREWORD i
INTRODUCTION iii
THE TESTIMONY OF JABU NKOSI v

SECTION A: Who and whose are you? xiv

CHAPTER ONE: The purpose of prayer 1
CHAPTER TWO: The Presence of God in every human body 21
CHAPTER THREE: What is a DNA or Deoxyribonucleic acid? 31
CHAPTER FOUR: You are trusted by God 47
CHAPTER FIVE: Nebucadnezzar you are flesh, your word is not the final word 53
CHAPTER SIX: Rejected and fallen 57

SECTION B: The power of the Word 70

CHAPTER SEVEN: Spiritual revolution 71
CHAPTER EIGHT: Do not forget what the enemy did to you 89
CHAPTER NINE: Valley experiences 97
CHAPTER TEN: God's Kairos revealed 109
CHAPTER ELEVEN: Your Appointed time 129
CHAPTER TWELVE: The shadow eclipsed the substance 139
CHAPTER THIRTEEN: Understanding the times ... 147
CHAPTER FOURTEEN: Power of attraction 157
CHAPTER FIFTEEN: Dual offices of the Messiah ... 167
CHAPTER SIXTEEN: Knowledge is a key 171

CHAPTER SEVENTEEN: The use of Anointing oil in prayer and warfare 179

SECTION C: Understanding the times of prayer and programming – Prayer watch **189**

CHAPTER EIGHTEEN: Night watches 193
CHAPTER NINETEEN: Day watches 217
CHAPTER TWENTY: Power of the Holy Communion 235
CHAPTER TWENTYONE: How to deal with accusations of the enemy in the place of work and in business 241

References **245**

ABOUT THE AUTHOR 246

FOREWORD

Pastor Portia has written a much needed book, this is the book to be read by generations. It's a kind of a book that must be passed on to the next generations. To alter the findings of recent discovery that declares that the life span of men is 54 years and women is 56 years in South Africa. God's desire for mankind is to have life full of prosperity and health up to 70 years and yonder.

Through the revealed Word of God and the Prayer Watch included in this book, we are challenged to give our lives to continuous prayer so that the verdict of the enemy over our lives and over our generation can be altered. The life span of this generation will be prolonged, and generations to come will find strength to deal with life threatening situations in their day as a result of our persistence in the word and prayer.

Mankind is threatened by many factors such as global-warming, global economic crash, incurable diseases and all these chaotic disasters that our world is facing today. Therefore, the magnitude of such knowledge is what the church needs to prevail for in times like these. Everything that the church needs is in God's word, and through understanding times and seasons of Prayer, we can be able to tap into eternity and the impact can be seen in our times and seasons.

I am blown away by Chapter 3, discovering that the ancient name of God; YHVH is engraved in every cell of our

Watch and Pray

bodies. I find this message so relevant to help this generation to deal with all kinds of blood diseases.

Congratulations to my daughter, Pastor Portia, GKWC is proud of you, and this book will be used by the Holy Spirit to change our world.

God bless you and increase you in knowledge and understanding of His word, for the edification of the church.

His Grace, Bishop BG Khumalo
God's Kingdom Worship Centre

"Bishop BG Khumalo sadly passed away in December 2019, five months before the release of this book. His legacy lives on. His Mantle shall be honoured by His Sons. We shall meet again in Glory! Shalom"

INTRODUCTION

There is more to creation than what meets the eye. There is more to Prayer than what the church practices. There is more to Christ's death and His resurrection than what we know and understand. There is more to life than what experience, background, religion and culture has taught us. There is a continued warfare in the realm of the spirit that affect the natural realm. Men ought to pray always and not get tired.

We are agents of change, invention and innovation. Every one of us has a prophetic directive and purpose of existence. It is our responsibility through intensive prayer and intercession to bring to pass the prophetic mandate and agenda of God concerning mankind. As individuals in our uniqueness, we have a powerful role to play to bring to pass the purpose, and the mission of God on the earth. The bible teaches us about a great man of prayer and intercession, his name was Simeon. He waited for the consolation of Israel and by the Holy Spirit it was made known to him that he will not die until he has seen the Messiah. He lived to see the manifestation of the promise of God, the same Grace is provided to this generation. Amen.

Watch and Pray

The words of this book are meant to deliver knowledge that will immediately provoke the Anointing, Grace and zeal to pray and refuse to settle for worry and unbelief. Our God is a mighty and powerful God, who lives outside time, He is the Creator and is not limited by any Laws that Govern creation. He is the great I AM, the Alpha and Omega. As you read the contents of this book, the Holy Spirit will reveal and advance the purpose for your life in your generation and beyond, and will direct you on how to pray and find establishment in His INFINITE GRACE.

BE BLESSED as you embark on the GREAT COMMISSION that will reveal the GREAT MISSION of God for your life.

God bless you!

THE TESTIMONY OF JABU NKOSI

My five-year-old daughter Renny, was diagnosed with Tuberculosis (TB) by a local clinic in Nelspruit. TB treatment was prescribed and administered to her with the hope of full recovery. It all started with swollenness around the throat area. Five months later the situation deteriorated; the treatment seemed not to make her better. The sores on the throat began to multiply, and she was eventually admitted at Themba Hospital. The biopsy was done on her and the results came revealing no disease, except Tuberculosis was found in her. But the shocking and frustrating thing was that the situation was worsening and my daughter's skin literally began to rot and peel off and stick on blankets and clothes.

We could not bathe her anymore, we ended up not putting clothes on her tiny body. Her strength and zeal to fight was slowly failing her as she began to throw up blood. She could not walk and play anymore like other kids, her immune system seemed to be shutting down. The doctors noticed her deteriorating situation and recommended that she should be transferred to Steve Biko Hospital for further tests and diagnosis.

Watch and Pray

Indeed, my daughter was transferred and tests were administered again, and I was informed that my daughter has lymphoma cancer. Steve Biko Hospital officials sent me for counselling sessions in order to prepare me for the life changing discovery and the new journey ahead of us. Having to learn how to deal with the condition of my daughter, was overwhelming and frightening. This cancer had attacked her immune system, and she was now transferred to a cancer ward. In a short space of time, her condition became worse, and she was then transferred to the intensive care unit. I can vividly remember pipes and machines all over my baby's tiny body.

Throughout this situation, many voices were echoing through my ears and thoughts. Some were telling me to sue the department of health for the misdiagnosis that was done and the Tuberculosis medication that was prescribed and administered already on my daughter. Some of our caring friends and relatives advised us to seek council from traditional healers. At that moment I realised that in times of need, it is very easy to backslide and try everything that friends and family members suggest. What I have learnt throughout this experience was; "Which report will I believe?" And what kind of help do I need? If you are not sure of what you want, any advice is the right one. I made a choice to swift through advises being offered by many people who cared for me and my daughter. This was a crucial time for my faith and my prayer life. I had to recognise the time and season that my life was in and remember that nothing is permanent in life. I encouraged myself by confessing that this situation will pass and one day I will testify and help someone in a similar situation.

Testimony of Jabu Nkosi

I had to resign from work so I can be available full time for my daughter. I needed to hear the inner voice of the Holy Spirit guiding me in the midst of this storm. I had to win the battle in the spirit and subject my thoughts and emotions to what the Word of God was saying to me. I made a conscious decision to believe the Word of God. When God said, I send my Word and heal them, I had no other option but to capture that Word, believe that Word, confess that Word, and sing that Word

As I focused on building my faith, my miracle did not immediately manifest, but this time I became strong for my daughter, and I began to be tenacious in my faith. I thought that my persistent faith will immediately change things around. Well, it did not work as anticipated. Actually, I realised that the firm faith was needed for me more than it was needed for my daughter. God needed me to be strong, stable and focused for the battle ahead, which was not yet revealed. I thought the diagnosis was the worst thing that could happen to me and my daughter…just stay on as we share our experience in this journey to total healing.

The Hospital recommended that my daughter start with chemotherapy immediately. I was informed that the cancer had spread all over her body. So they had to insert a port-a-cath device under her skin to transfer medication to fight the cancer cells and reduce cancer symptoms. I consented to the procedure with the hope that the treatment will work and we will soon go home.

Then…The worst thing happened!

Watch and Pray

The hospital called to inform me that my daughter had passed away, my entire being crushed! With the little strength I had, I made my way to the hospital ward where she was being treated, and when I reached the ward, they had already disconnected the life support machine. Her tiny body was already wrapped and ready to be dispatched to the mortuary. They informed me that they did all they could but they failed, the Morgue number allocated for my daughter's body was 248. The mortuary stretcher was in the ward to collect my daughter's body, the hospital staff was kind enough to comfort me and try to make me feel better. I was overwhelmed as I watched the mortuary stretcher leave the ward carrying her body. I realised that my daughter is going to a place where her dreams and desires will never come to pass. As the elevator doors opened, I recognised its sound, my mind became alert and realised that indeed she is gone. At that moment, I had to say my final goodbyes to my beloved daughter.

I shouted, bring her back! I need to say goodbye. I need three minutes of your time. I need to at least pray for her and release her. They honoured my request and brought her back. I began to pray in tongues, I did not know what I wanted to say to God. To this day, I do not remember my prayer. All I needed to do was to pray, and I felt the peace of God inside of me.

Then the Unthinkable happened, Hallelujah!

I heard my daughter shout, "Mama!"

The doctors and the mortuary officials that came to collect my daughter's body shouted back and said, "Oh! She is alive." As they were shouting I was full of the power to pray and

Testimony of Jabu Nkosi

worship God. I found myself praying in the dispensary and moving around the hospital, the security guards were calling each other to halt me, when they tried to touch me, they could not touch me, the anointing was so heavy on me. They injected me to calm me down and sleep but the injection never worked. I never slept. I received more anointing to worship and pray, my child never went to the morgue, she was indeed alive! I remembered the testimony of Lazarus, Jesus called him out of the tomb, even after Martha declared him to be smelling. He rose from the dead to the table, and he indeed dined with the Lord. Many came to see he who was dead and now alive. What a mighty God we serve. He did it for me, he can do it for anyone who comes to Him believing that He is able to do anything.

But, it was not over yet...

My daughter was kept in hospital for observation and further tests after God brought her back to life. Two weeks later they put her in the isolation ward because the doctors realised that the type of cancer found in her blood was still there. In everything, I learnt that the tongue is powerful, just as the Bible declares, life and death is in the power of your tongue and those who love it will eat its fruits. The enemy was provoking me to confess what my eyes were seeing and what the doctors were saying. I learnt not to speak what I do not want to see. It may be in your mind, but do not confess it. Confession is confirmation, and confirmation brings possession. In the cancer ward where we were, most mothers spoke with their own mouths and confessed that their children were dying and their children did indeed die. The pain you see

Watch and Pray

in your child must not tempt you to hand them over to the grave through confession of what you see and feel. I had to fight for my child. I knew that her life was depending on my faith.

Things in the natural were not clear, I did not know whether I would come out victorious or defeated in this battle.

As months went by, I realised that my daughter was getting blind as she was taking chemotherapy again. The functioning of her body ceased. She also stopped speaking. The only way I could see that she was alive was through the tears that were dripping from her eyes. The hospital officials counselled me, and also informed me that her voice box was damaged, and therefore, she will never be able to speak again. I had to take two weeks of fasting and prayer to hear guidance from the Lord about my situation. After two weeks my daughter called me, "mama", her voice returned back to her, hallelujah. What does not happen with doctors, happens with God.

Just when I was thinking things were getting better…

I was again informed that my daughter will never walk again, a wheelchair from the Mpumalanga Health Department was organised as support to move my daughter around for when we returned home in Nelspruit. I told the hospital staff who delivered the news that, I was enough with hearing all these news and that only God could confirm my daughter's sudden paralysis. I told them that what they were telling me were only mere medical facts, but God was the only one to confirm the truth of my daughter's condition.

Testimony of Jabu Nkosi

Christmas season came and my daughter was released for seasonal holidays and the hospital provided us with a temporal wheelchair. And when my employer heard that we were coming home, they also donated a wheelchair. My daughter had two wheelchairs and the enemy was preaching in my mind saying I must accept her paralysis. Saying, "Look, you even have two wheelchairs for her now."

Our holiday season from the hospital started around the 15th of December 2011 and ended on the 3rd of January 2012. We enjoyed being in a familiar environment though my daughter was now blind and confined to a wheel chair. I decided to focus on building my faith for the next miracle. I refused to be discouraged, and I thought the starting point should be watching sermons and reading the bible. While watching sermons on TV and miracles performed on TV services, I desired to be at one of those services with my daughter to receive our miracle. As I was desiring and talking to myself, a voice answered me, "Have you forgotten? She was dead and now she is alive. You can also lay hands on her and pray, she will recover." The voice called me again in my spirit and said; "I want to show you my power". I then began to pray in the spirit. And one day around the 27th December 2011, while I was bathing my daughter, I stepped out to pick clothes for her. To my surprise and amazement, while choosing her clothes, I heard her speak to me saying, Mummy, *"I don't like the dress you picked for me"*. I felt disoriented by her statement, because she is supposed to be blind, so, how did she see the dress I picked for her? I asked her, how do you know which dress I picked for you? She said I can see the dress, change it to this one. I immediately praised Jehovah Rapha

Watch and Pray

who continues to heal our diseases. I began to believe that the conversation I had within me was actually a conversation with the Lord.

My daughter said to me, "Mama, I am tired of this wheel chair". While listening to her, I then stepped outside to spill the bathing water. When I returned, I found her standing and her body was shaking. There she was, very excited and she said, "Mama, look at me I can stand." Instead of being filled with joy, I got scared as I remembered the doctor's instruction about how to handle her and the port that was inserted in her flesh. I was clearly told to ensure that she is fastened at all times on the wheel chair, and that the port cannot move, and if that happen she may die. She began to walk with her toes as she was shaking.

She took three steps and she fell and the worst thing that I thought could happen to her didn't happen. I started praying in tongues. I went outside around the house amazed at what just happened in the house. Since that day, my daughter walked, and there was no longer need for a wheel chair. I knew God was able to do it for me, but I was not ready or expecting it to happen at that speed. It was in January 2012, when we went back to the hospital after our Christmas holidays. I walked into the hospital with her walking and not on the wheel chair. When the doctor recognized my daughter, he became afraid seeing her walking. He called me into his office and confessed that this was indeed a miracle child. And he said to me from today, before I touch my child I must pray and thank God for her life.

Testimony of Jabu Nkosi

My daughter continued with her chemotherapy as an outpatient, and the tests were ran on her to determine the impact of the treatment. After a few months we received the test results, and she was declared cancer free. As I write this, it has been seven years, since she is cancer free. She is now a healthy and a strong young girl, who is currently at school in grade six (6).

.

Watch and Pray

SECTION A:

WHO AND WHOSE ARE YOU?

CHAPTER ONE

THE PURPOSE OF PRAYER

And I will give unto thee the keys of the kingdom of heaven: and whatsoever thou shalt bind on earth shall be bound in heaven: and whatsoever thou shalt loose on earth shall be loosed in heaven" (Matthew 16:9 BSB).

"The highest heavens belong to the LORD, but the earth He has given to mankind" (Psalm 115:16 BSB).

Why should we pray?

Luke 18:1- 8: The parable of a persistent widow

Then He spoke a parable to them, that men always ought to pray and not lose heart, saying: "There was in a certain city a judge who did not fear God nor regard man. Now there was a widow in that city; and she came to him, saying, "Get justice for me from my adversary." And he would not for a while; but afterward he said within himself, 'Though I do not fear God nor regard man, yet because this widow troubles me I will avenge her, lest by her continual coming she weary me.' " Then

Watch and Pray

the Lord said, "Hear what the unjust judge said. And shall God not avenge His own elect who cry out day and night to Him though He bears long with them? I tell you that He will avenge them speedily. Nevertheless, when the Son of Man comes, will He really find faith on the earth?"

When a woman conceive a baby, it simply means God released His Spirit into the womb of a woman using the contact of a woman's eggs and a man's seed. The spirit comes from God. The eggs and the seed of a man will receive life and the baby is knitted in the womb of the mother. The child will become spirit living in a body with a soul. Now as we grow physically we need to build our lives, get jobs, and income to survive on earth. But our spirit hosted by our physical body must also grow and be fed with spiritual food. Moreover, your soul and spirit must be born again. And your spirit needs to be fed spiritual food which is the Word of God that leads to exercising faith. You enforce your faith by sending vibrations and power through declarations and prayer to the spirit world that will manifest in the natural by affecting your environment. The Spirit beings cannot fight and win spiritual battles using physical methods and strategies. You will need to read and study the word, hear the word, pray the word and confess the word of God. Let me use the testimony of Daniel in the book of Daniel 9:2 to qualify the context; "In the first year of his reign, I, Daniel, understood from the books the number of years which, according to the word of the Lord to Jeremiah the prophet, must pass before desolations which had been pronounced on Jerusalem would end; and it was seventy years. So I directed my attention to the Lord God to seek Him in prayer and supplication, with fasting, sackcloth and ashes.

The Purpose of Prayer

"And whiles I was speaking, and praying, and confessing my sin and the sin of my people Israel, and presenting my supplication before the Lord my God for the holy mountain of my God; Yea, whiles I was speaking in prayer, even the man Gabriel, whom I had seen in the vision at the beginning, being caused to fly swiftly, touched me about the time of the evening oblation. And he informed me, and talked with me, and said, O Daniel, I am now come forth to give thee skill and understanding" (Daniel 9:20 – 22 KJV).

"Then said he unto me, Fear not, Daniel: for from the first day that thou didst set thine heart to understand, and to chasten thyself before thy God, thy words were heard, and I am come for thy words. But the prince of the kingdom of Persia withstood me one and twenty days: but, lo, Michael, one of the chief princes, came to help me; and I remained there with the kings of Persia. Now I am come to make thee understand what shall befall thy people in the latter days: for yet the vision is for many days" (Daniel 10:12-14 KJV).

Jurisdiction Matters

When you give something to someone you relinquish your control over it. You keep your opinion to yourself unless you are requested to make input. Psalm 115 tells us that the highest heavens belong to God and the earth He has given to the sons of men. Adam as the father of mankind decided to bring in another ruler upon the earth. He might have not been aware of the implications of disobedience when he was eating the forbidden fruit at that time. But the repercussions of his disobedience have eternal impact, unless men receive Christ Jesus as the Lord and Saviour they have no escape. Therefore,

Watch and Pray

God will not intervene in the affairs of men unless men pray. Because prayer is a way of asking God to intervene in one's affairs.

The earth is under men's jurisdiction. Mankind can invite any spirit they want and the spirits respond to men's invitation particularly within their jurisdiction, regardless of the spirit's being good or evil. The testimony of Daniel becomes evident that men ought to pray to receive divine intervention. The earth belongs to men. Spirit must contend to gain access to the land of the mortals. Therefore, our prayers give angels full access to come and intervene in the affairs of men. Imagine with me, if Daniel did not pray for understanding and the release of Israel, do you think Israel would have been released on time? Do you think Angels would have decided to come without invitation to fulfil the word of prophesy? I believe God will always need a man to work with on earth. Even if God was to intervene without the prayers of men, when things begin to happen, man may not have understanding of what to do and that may end up in wasted energy and effort.

We pray to seek God's Intervention

When Jesus taught His disciples how to pray he said:

Our Father, which art in heaven, Hallowed be thy Name. Thy Kingdom come. Thy will be done in earth, as it is in heaven. Give us this day our daily bread. And forgive us our trespasses, as we forgive them that trespass against us. And lead us not into temptation, but deliver us from evil. For thine is the kingdom, the power, and the glory, For ever and ever. Amen. (See Matthew 6:9-13 KJV).

The Purpose of Prayer

Jesus was teaching the disciples about the Power of Prayer that ushers in the presence that is not limited by what limits mankind. Men can depend on God because He is dependable. Moreover, the sons of men should engage God and seek intervention from him and grow in the relationship with him and call Him, Father. Not just father but Heavenly Father. Meaning, You are my Father and You are not bound by time and forces of gravity because You reside outside of all of these things and You created everything seen and unseen. You sustain everything by your word. You are Holy, meaning You are different. You are invisible yet your works are visible. You make yourself visible to whoever You choose to, and You decide how to make Yourself known, and You remain the same yesterday, today and forever regardless of recognition or worship from your creation.

Mankind can seek the Father's intervention on the following:

- **Daily provision** – give us this day our daily bread. We need not to depend upon our limited abilities and salaries for daily supply. God, as our Heavenly Father finds pleasure in us asking and trusting Him for provision and He finds pleasure in supplying our daily needs. The daily provisions of God are not limited to bread and water but include also the very air we breathe, health, and sound mind. Think of what we need to live each day. We need oxygen, we need our bodies to be functional, we need our brain to communicate soundly with our body and many other significant needs for our everyday provisions, Hallelujah. He loads us with daily benefits!

Watch and Pray

- **Forgiveness of sin** – God through Jesus Christ has provided a way of escape for our sins. We know the devil is the accuser of brethren but the blood of Jesus Christ silences the voice of accusation. Therefore, when we come to Him in repentance and confessing our sins, he forgives us our transgressions and redeems us from the accuser.
- **Perfect will of God** - As it is happening in heaven to also happen on earth and in our lives. We understand that in heaven there's no pain, sorrow and poverty. We can pray for the manifestation of the kingdom of God and His will in our lives and our homes. His will is for us to conquer; defeat is not of God. And His will, will always prevail in the lives of His children.
- The presence of the kingdom and rulership of heaven to prevail over the affairs of men, families and nations.
- Deliverance and protection from powers above our strength, He promises deliverance from temptations and evil. The Lord's promises are "Yes and Amen".
- Confidence in God as we worship Him for who He is in our lives.

We are at WAR

There are many different types of warfare the living faces, whether they are believers or not. Whether we are aware of it or not, whether we want to fight or not, the enemy is fighting every individual that is born of a woman. Some battles we win, some we lose. But in prayer, we are sure of victory because Jesus Christ overcame the world.

The Purpose of Prayer

Some of the Warfare faced by people

- Spiritual Warfare

Is a battle taking place in the spiritual realm, this battle can be fought and won in prayer. Men ought to pray and win battles in the spirit so that they can experience physical victory.

"For though we walk in the flesh, we do not war after the flesh: (For the weapons of our warfare are not carnal, but mighty through God to the pulling down of strong holds;) Casting down imaginations, and every high thing that exalteth itself against the knowledge of God, and bringing into captivity every thought to the obedience of Christ" (2 Corinthians 10:3-5 KJV)

In Ephesians 6: 10 Paul encourages believers to be strong in the Lord and in the power of His Mighty. He further admonishes believers to put on the whole armour of God to be able to stand against the wiles of the devil.

He further admonishes believers to take unto them the whole armour of God, that they may be able to withstand in the evil day, and having done all, to stand.

- Gird your Loins with Truth, and have the breastplate of righteousness
- Their feet Shod with the preparation of the gospel of peace
- Above all, taking the shield of faith to quench all the fiery darts of the wicked
- Take the helmet of salvation, and the sword of the spirit, which is the word of God

Watch and Pray

- Pray always as the Spirit leads, pray in other tongues, watching with perseverance and supplication for all saints

I) Physical Warfare

Dictionary.com defines Physical Warfare as the process of military struggle between two nations or groups of nations;

Or armed conflict between two massed enemies, armies, or the like. Or conflict, especially between vicious and unrelenting competitors or political rivals.

II) Biological Warfare

According to Wikipedia, Biological warfare (BW) — also known as germ warfare — is the use of biological toxins or infectious agents such as bacteria, viruses, insects, and fungi with the intent to kill or incapacitate humans, animals or plants as an act of war. Biological weapons (often termed "bio-weapons", "biological threat agents", or "bio-agents") are living organisms or replicating entities (viruses, which are not universally considered "alive"). Entomological (insect) warfare is a subtype of Biological Warfare.

Biological warfare is distinct from nuclear warfare and chemical warfare, which together with biological warfare make up NBC, the military initialism for nuclear, biological, and chemical warfare using weapons of mass destruction (WMDs). None of these are considered conventional weapons, which are deployed primarily for their explosive, kinetic, or incendiary potential.

The Purpose of Prayer

Biological weapons may be employed in various ways to gain a strategic or tactical advantage over the enemy, either by threats or by actual deployments. Like some chemical weapons, biological weapons may also be useful as area denial weapons. These agents may be lethal or non-lethal, and may be targeted against a single individual, a group of people, or even an entire population

iii) What is Psychological Warfare?

Psychological warfare is a broad term, but in all documented cases, the concept uses actions intended to reduce an opponent's morale or mental well-being. The aim is to use manipulative tactics to intimidate or persuade a person or people. This process is usually employed through propaganda. Propaganda is ideas or statements that are false or exaggerated and is deliberately spread to influence the masses. The goal of psychological warfare is to intentionally use propaganda to manipulate another and break down their will without using physical force.

To get a clearer picture, let's take a look at some techniques that have been used throughout history.

Techniques

Psychological warfare uses fear to break down the psychological well-being of an opponent. Look at the list below for techniques that can be used to spread psychological uncertainty, fear, and terror.

Watch and Pray

- **News Outlets and Social Media Platforms**: The news is a large information source that all can tap into. The news has the ability to spread whichever information it chooses. By infiltrating a news source, a population could be tainted by volatile information.
- **Threats**: Threats of violence, restrictions of freedom, and control can be made to instil fear in the people. These could be empty threats or threats with true intention. Whatever the case, threatening a group or groups of people can psychologically damage the recipients over time, putting them in a state of constant fear, anxiety, and terror.
- **Leaflets**: Leaflets are pieces of paper with manipulative messages/pictures that are dropped from the air over areas of war or political unrest. The goal is to persuade the recipients to either support or oppose the political event taking place.
- **Objects**: Using objects such as t-shirts, posters, hats, pins, and more is an effective way to get a message across. The objects can become symbols for larger messages regarding politics, radical beliefs, religious philosophies, etc. These objects can become tools for promotion and even worship.
- **False flag**: A false flag is when a group releases false information or carries out a fake terror attack to instil fear in people. However, the blame is put on another group or organization to gain control over the masses and shift opinion.
- **Media**: While it may not seem like it, films, music, and books can act as tools for psychological warfare. The

The Purpose of Prayer

messages in media can rewrite history from a new perspective and/or put new ideas in the minds of the populous

iii) Technological Warfare

From cyber-attacks to robotic weapons, twenty-first century war is increasingly disembodied as Artificial Intelligence is deployed globally. Our wars are being fought in the atmosphere of information, technology and by machines. And yet our conscience of war is stuck in the pre-digital age.

We're used to thinking of war as a physical phenomenon, as an outbreak of destructive violence that takes place in the physical world. Bullets fly, bombs explode, tanks roll, people collapse. Technological warfare informs the future of warfare; Wikipedia defines a drone strike as an attack by one or more unnamed combat aerial vehicles or weaponized commercial unmanned aerial vehicles. For unmanned combat aerial vehicles, an attack usually involves firing a missile or releasing a bomb at a target.

It is important for the believers to understand that there are different types of warfare, and we must be able to reconcile Physical, Biological, Psychological and Technological to Spiritual Warfare. God in His infinite mercies has given us the weapons that aren't seen with the natural eyes. But our weapons are not of this world, they're powerful to paralyse and nullify the attacks of the enemy. All warfare be it Physical, Psychological, Technological or Biological is conceived in the spirit and manifest in the natural realm. The parable of the widow woman demonstrates the power of persistent prayers.

Watch and Pray

She refused to be silenced by the status of her widowhood. She continued to approach the evil judge and demanded justice against her adversaries. Because of her continuous persistence, her desires were granted. Persistence demonstrates the life of a believer who has faith in God. When we persist in prayer and persevere, we resist the verdict of our current situation. Prayer and faith are a weapon that assures results and the enemy gets irritated when he is resisted, so he flees from the scene. Like the widow woman, these are some of the weapons that we have at our disposal:

- Persistence in Prayer
- Issuing declarations and decrees aligned to the Word of God
- The Name of Jesus Christ
- The Blood of Jesus Christ
- The Communion Meal
- Creation and its elements such as, lightening, water, earth, moon, sun and stars.
- The winds of the Lord, East Wind, West Wind, North Wind and South Wind

Ephesian 6:12 reminds us of the warfare we are in. The warfare we are in is not carnal or physical but rather spiritual. For we wrestle not against flesh and blood, but against principalities, against powers, against the rulers of the darkness of this world, against spiritual wickedness in high places.

Our struggles may look natural or physical but they are not, our struggles may look like it's against people but they're not. Our warfare is against:

The Purpose of Prayer

- Principalities
- Powers
- Rulers of darkness
- Spiritual wickedness in high places

Principalities

Principalities in biblical times was known as a state ruled by a prince, or a governor and was usually a relatively small state or a state that falls within a larger state or nation such as in the Roman Empire. It can be that which holds or has held rule over a population that is either republics or principalities. Taken as it is, a principality can have dominion within the confines of a larger dominion or rule. From the description above we understand that our warfare is against a prince of a kingdom, Princes also have an entourage accompanying them in battle. You may be looking like you are alone in battle against Princes or governors, but Jehovah Saboath, the Lord of Host is with you in battle against princes, Hallelujah.

Powers

Powers are those that hold power within a kingdom, a principality, or even an empire. This could be wielded by kings or emperors, like King Nebuchadnezzar, he held absolute power over the kingdom of Babylon. For example, a local power means to have the ability or capacity to act or do something effectively exerting control, influence, creating and enforcing laws or authority over people or nation. There are key people in positions of power and influence and you know

Watch and Pray

very well that as long as they are still occupying certain positions of influence it will be almost impossible for you to breakthrough. They will be blocking your ways, and ideas to an extent of stealing your initiatives and implementing them as their own and not give credit where it is due.

For victory to be realised, we need to go beyond people. We must understand that the influence of spirits on people is real and deep. Spirits possess influence and use human vessels to get to us. If we see attacks by such people as natural battles and take them personal, then we are far from winning the battle. Do not address the wrong enemy. Unmask the enemy through prayer. Your real enemy is a Spirit that enters and controls people in positions of power and influence. Victory is possible, see through the enemy that is disguising itself and address it without fear.

Rulers of darkness

These spirits are operating over a specific Province or Territory in a Country. It is easy to tell if fallen angels are in control by looking at what is going on in that particular Province, Place or Territory. We have unexercised dominion over these spirits. We learn from scripture that Saul was on his way to Damascus to effect the desired outcomes outlined in a letter to arrest, afflict and kill Christians in this particular territory. He had a mission to wipe out the new church. It is evident that the church was prayerful and Jesus intervened on Saul's way to Damascus.

Jesus met Saul on the way. That encounter changed everything, and the Spirit of a ruler submitted to the ancient of

The Purpose of Prayer

days. Blind as he was after the light from heaven flashed around him. He fell to the ground and heard a voice speak to him; Saul's conversion came and the ordinary man named Ananias of Damascus ministered by the Holy Spirit to Saul. We see in this great chapter of the book of Acts 9 that creation in a form of light cooperated with the church and the church prevailed over the intentions and expectations of the enemy that was using Saul. He thought he was doing the Lord's service by persecuting the Church. It is evident that men are vessels and are used by spirits. It depends which spirit you will open yourself to.

Spiritual Wickedness in High places

The last group mentioned is "spiritual wickedness" in high places. The High Places refers to the dwelling place of God as well as the abode of angels and evil spirits.

The American Heritage Dictionary Thesaurus defines Wicked – Wickedness:

Morally bad in nature or practice. Adj wrong, wicked, immoral, iniquitous, base, vile, evil, black-hearted, evil-minded, sinful, depraved, dissolute, reprehensible, and blameworthy.

"When the unclean spirit is gone out of a man, he walketh through dry places, seeking rest, and findeth none. 44 Then he saith, I will return into my house from whence I came out; and when he is come, he findeth it empty, swept, and garnished. 45 Then goeth he, and taketh with himself seven other spirits more wicked than himself, and they enter in and dwell there: and the last state of that man is worse than the first. Even so shall it be also unto this wicked generation." (Matthew 12:43-45 KJV).

Watch and Pray

"And he was casting out a devil, and it was dumb. And it came to pass, when the devil was gone out, the dumb spake; and the people wondered. 15 But some of them said, He casteth out devils through Beelzebub the chief of the devils" (Luke 11:14-15 KJV).

These category of Spirits possess people or animals. These evil spirits are responsible for inflicting pain, causing diseases, mental problems and other problems experienced by people. There are many instances of Jesus "casting" spirits out of people. He even allowed Legion to go into a herd of swine that ran off a cliff" (See Mark 5:1-13).

A person's body is like a house, housing your spirit and has rooms to house other Spirits. As believers, when we are born again we receive the Holy Spirit and other Spiritual gifts that are housed in our bodies. Evil Spirits, also seek to be housed in people's bodies. All spirits need a human body to be able to operate on earth. Believers must do a spring cleaning of their bodies on a regular basis to check who is occupying the other rooms in their bodies.

Prayer brings Revelation

Many things are hidden from the natural eye, the Holy Spirit through prayer reveals the true enemy and empowers us to resist and trample upon him.

People in our inner circle may appear to love us, but the truth of their love can only be revealed through prayer. Even Judas and Simon Peter declared their love for Jesus. The question is, if that love can be tested, can it stand the test of time? If your friends or family can be promised what they regard as core in their lives in exchange of giving you up, can

The Purpose of Prayer

they protect you? You can only know that by revelation. And a prayer less person cannot get accurate revelation instead a familiar spirit will take over and deceive them.

Jesus said to his beloved Judas, I know you will betray me to the hands of sinners, to Peter He said before a rooster crows you will disown me three times. (See Matthew 26:34) but Jesus continued to love them and manage them with great wisdom. Many people died in the hands of their enemies without knowing that they're their enemies.

Let us watch and pray always. For the enemy is working overtime to take as many people as possible to hell. Prayer keeps us vigilant as we wait for the call of the Master. Prayer keeps us focused on our assignment and make us able to win battles in our lifetime and leave behind footprints of victory for those coming after us. Jesus said, I will give you the keys of the Kingdom of heaven and the gates of your enemies and hell will not prevail against you. No one will be able to stand against you in this season, as the Lord was with Joshua, He is with you today. The Jericho walls will fall before you, the overflowing river will open up for you. Hallelujah!

Prayer Points to set the scene and stir the supernatural in us.

1. Lord Jesus, I receive you in my heart as my personal Lord and Saviour, I confess with my mouth that you came down and you died for the sins of the world and you rose again.

2. I acknowledge my sins and the sins of my Fathers, I ask you to forgive me and accept me in your kingdom.

Watch and Pray

3. Give me your Holy Spirit to help me in my weaknesses and to teach me all things concerning the Kingdom of God.

4. Lord, do not lead me to temptation but deliver me from the evil one,

5. I receive your provision in my life and destiny in Jesus Name.

6. I receive the weapons of my warfare to fight a good fight of Faith in my life.

7. I speak to my feet, and command them to carry me to the right places, and refuse to take me to a place where my life and destiny will be assassinated in Jesus Mighty name.

8. I reject any arrow of the enemy fired against my life and family in Jesus Mighty name.

9. Any Biological Weapon carrying viruses, bacteria's, insects, and fungi with the intent to kill or incapacitate people, I paralyse your intent and strike your eyes with blindness, and wipe out your name from under the sun in the name of Jesus Christ.

10. I render powerless any technological weapon, be it robots, drones, and any form of artificial intelligence sent against my life, destiny and family. I delete the records in the realm of the Spirit, air, the water and land in the name of Jesus.

11. I rise against any spirit that assassinate character, dignity and integrity. Any lies circulated through media,

The Purpose of Prayer

social, visual and audio, I scatter them in the name of Jesus Christ. I assassinate the assassin in the name of Jesus Christ.

12. I rise against the Principalities, Rulers, Powers and Spirit of Wickedness in High Places in the name of Jesus Christ. I receive the wisdom to discern the battle and receive weapons relevant for every battle in Jesus name.

13. I receive the anointing and the grace to persist and persevere in prayer. I refuse to give up. I receive the wisdom to use my shield of Faith to quench the fiery darts of the enemy.

14. I receive the bread which is the body of my Lord Jesus and I receive the Cup which is the blood of Jesus Christ. As I partake of this communion meal, He increases in my life and everything else decreases in the name of Jesus.

15. I speak to the name of God in my blood cells to arise and fight any virus, bacteria, inherited diseases and any form of biological weapon fired against my blood type in Jesus name. I cover my life and my family with the blood of Jesus Christ. I declare Psalm 91 over everything that concerns me.

16. As Moses stretched out his hand over the sea; and the Lord caused the sea to go back by a strong east wind all that night, and made the sea dry land, and the waters were divided. And the children of Israel went into the midst of the sea upon dry ground; the waters were a

Watch and Pray

wall unto them on their right and left hand. I rise, and command the east wind to blow over my family and nation, and make a way for us where there seem to be no way.

17. I command the "East Wind" to rise and overthrow any weapons fashioned against my life, family, church and nation in Jesus Mighty name.

Begin to thank the Lord for Victory over your battles. You are more than a conqueror because Jesus conquered. Read Psalm 103

Shalom, Shalom as we continue to watch and pray!

CHAPTER TWO

THE PRESENCE OF GOD IN EVERY HUMAN BODY

In the eternity beginning Elohim was, and in the beginning Elohim created heaven and earth. Heaven and earth are the work of His wonderful hands. God did not originally reside in heaven; He was there before; the heaven was created by Him. He spoke all things that were not into being and they became and He sustained everything by the same word he used to create. What a Mighty God we serve. After all His good works, He needed someone like Him to look after the earth and the creation He had created.

"Then Elohim said, "Let us make man in our image, after our likeness. And let them have dominion over the fish of the sea and over the birds of the heavens and over the livestock and over all the earth and over every creeping thing that creeps on the earth" (Genesis 1:26 KJV).

"God formed man of the dust of the ground, and breathed into his nostrils the breath of life, and man became a living soul" (Genesis 2:7"). It was on the sixth day of creation when Elohim created man. He took the earthly material which was the dust of the ground and God breathed His Spirit into man and man became a living soul. Before the breath of Elohim was breathed into man, the body of a Man remained a dead corpse. God imparted his breath into the body of a Man and blood was formed and man received life. We can conclude that blood is the evidence and manifestation of life. For the life of a thing is in its blood. Man became a dual being, a spirit with a soul residing in a body.

Interpretation of a dual being

The breath released by God into the body of a man contained words or rather activated words that are existing in every DNA of a human being. We are made of God's words. God made a human mind to be a reservoir of words. The very words that fill our minds, are the very same words that fill every cell in our body. There is an effective communication taking place from the brain filtering the human body. Our body system is created in such a manner that there is congruence and proper communication that takes place within ourselves. And this communication goes beyond ourselves into the next generation of our offspring.

When God wants to heal us from sickness, He first sends His Word to minister and activate our spirit and faith. The mind becomes persuaded and agrees with our spirit and the body manifests the healing. That is why it is very important to receive and believe every Word declared upon your life by God through the ministers of His Word. When God wants to do something new in a nation, community, church or family, He sends a prophet to announce and declare the season of change

The Presence of God in every Human Body

and the appointed time. The first action that takes place is a spoken and received Word.

Have you noticed that a curse is a spoken word over a person's life, as a result of unhappiness from the heart and mouth of the person of authority over someone's life? The same happens with a blessing. A blessing is a spoken word from a satisfied, moved and merry heart of a person with authority over someone's life. People's lives and destinies are tied to spoken words. Our spirit being is conscious of spoken words far better than our physical being. Our physical being is influenced more by senses and feelings than words. When a blessing or a curse is spoken, it is not necessarily referred to your physicality, it is actually addressing your spirit being. No wonder blessings and curses are transferable to those that are connected to us by blood or covenant. According to my interpretation of the law of life, spirituality rules the natural. Whatever battle I win or lose in the spirit, it is likely to be won or lost in the natural realm.

See the scripture below:

When Israel was about to die, he called all his sons to come and hear words of what will befall them in the near future.

"And Jacob called unto his sons, and said, gather yourselves together, that I may tell you that which shall befall you in the last days. Gather yourselves together, and hear, ye sons of Jacob; and hearken unto Israel your father" (Genesis 49:1-2 KJV).

Watch and Pray

Reuben the first born of his father.

"Reuben, thou art my firstborn, my might, and the beginning of my strength, the excellency of power, unstable as water, thou shall not excel; because thou went up to your father's bed; then defiled thou it; he went up to my couch" (Genesis 49:3-4 KJV).

As a result of this spoken word, Reuben remained average and without excellence in his projects even after Moses the man of God came to rewrite his destiny and purpose. No one from the lineage of Reuben became kings or priests, yet he was a first born son. He was reduced from excellency to average.

Reuben was the firstborn son of Jacob and Leah. He was waiting in great anticipation for the blessing of his great father. The declaration started well as it declared what a firstborn should be to his father.

- **The Father's Might** – meaning, you Reuben are the tangible and undeniable evidence that I, your father am fruitful and able to procreate. You are my miracle and testimony that I am able to bear children.
- **The beginning of my strength** – I am encouraged to procreate because you Reuben proved that I have it within myself to do it, you are the beginning of my victories, the beginning of progress.
- **The excellency of power** – you prevailed and confirmed the prophecy of God to my grandfather Abraham that a nation is in me, how excellent are you my son.

The Presence of God in every Human Body

BUT...

- You are unstable and turbulent as water, you are wavering, you cannot be trusted, you are not trustworthy, you think with your emotions, you do not apply your mind and reason. You certainly do not respect what is not yours. Moments of temporary pleasure controls you, you are not like your brother Joseph, who revered God even in secret and ran away from Potiphar's wife. You were not arrested for your fornicators act, you thought you got away in the natural, but in the spirit you were arrested, and a verdict of being average was placed upon you and your descendants after you. Joseph was accused and arrested for the act of violating someone's wife, but in the spirit he was a free man, in the natural he was a slave prisoner. Because the spirit controls the natural, his spiritual freedom manifested in the natural and every accusation of the enemy had to submit to the freedom he earned in the spirit. The spirit testified of his innocence even though he was a foreign slave, and no man could speak for him and of his nobleness.
- Thou shall not excel —you will not surpass others, you will not shine or have dominion, you will not be the best in your skill, you will not gain pre-eminence, you will perform on average or satisfactory.
- You went knowingly up to my bed, you had intercourse with my woman and defiled my altar which is my bed, you engaged yourself into sexual immorality, you did not only defile yourself, you defiled my bed. How do I share a woman with my blood son?

Watch and Pray

These are the news from a dying Patriarch, a man of authority, a prophet of His household to his firstborn son. The son that might have not known that the Father knew all along what he did with his woman. Everything done in darkness has to come to light, and in this scenario it seems to be redirecting the destiny of this great man who was supposed to be the father's might, the beginning of the father's strength, and who was supposed to manifest excellence. I think within himself, Reuben wished he could reverse that moment. The pleasure moment has turned into a bitter taste, full of regret and jealousy, feeling like his blessed brothers are living the life that was supposed to be his.

Have you ever felt like Reuben, where you desire to reverse time and do something differently, and review your decisions?

There is still hope for Reuben

There is a Moses that God had sent in His great mercy to minister hope over his life. Mercy and Grace are granted, and another chance is freely given.

Everybody needs a prophet with spiritual authority to speak words into their lives and unlock ancient doors and gates of destiny. For us to progress, breakthrough and dominate our situation we should not be weary to speak the Word of God into our situations. Apprise yourself with the Word of God, so that when you pray, you speak the Word of God. Remember, the Word of God in your mouth carries the same power and authority as it does in God's mouth. What He is able to do with His spoken Word, you will be able to do the same with His word in your mouth, Amen. Genesis 1, tells us that the earth

The Presence of God in every Human Body

was void and without form, and God spoke things that were not, as though they were and they became. He declared what He wanted to see, not the disorder, darkness and the emptiness that was there. What your eyes see now is temporal, do not allow yourself to be discouraged by temporal situations in your life, they will surely pass away. And the Word of God declared in faith will outlive the situations you face today, and God's Word in your mouth is eternal and it always prevails.

He sent His Word.

Are you having a pressing situation in your life? Do you desire a turnaround? Are you sick in your body? Do you know that the Holy Spirit is forever present in every situation? He is forever brooding over your situation waiting for you to speak the creating Word of God, and your expectations shall be granted in Jesus name. This is what *Jesus said to us, "Ask anything in my name, and I will do it" (John 14:14 NKJV).*

The starting point of dealing with every mess is to speak to the messy situation, and create what you would like to exchange it for, like God did in Genesis 1. God saw the formless and dark earth. And God said, I am exchanging this darkness for light, I am exchanging this formlessness for order, and there it was. And God saw the light, that it was good and God divided the light from darkness. And called the light, day, and called the darkness, night. And the evening and morning was the first day. God spoke His word to heal, create and restore his order upon the earth.

Watch and Pray

Are you sick in your body?

Speak and command the cells in your body to fight against sickness and diseases. Trade in your sickness for health at the altar of prayer. Did you know that the cells in your body are actually soldiers that guard your body from attacks? God has given you soldiers inside your body system, and you must issue a command of action, and the soldier's in your body shall cooperate with you. Your cells must not hear strange voices, in Jesus name! After you have commanded your situation, allow your spirit to see the good thing you have declared coming to pass. Bring a division also or a separation of light and darkness in the affairs of your life. You cannot praise God for the manifestation and be entertaining the enemy on the other side.

Power of Naming

After God declared what He wanted to see, He spoke not what was happening at that time. God named the miracle of light, Day, and he brought division between light and darkness. The two cannot share space. Name your Miracle, protect your miracle and do not allow it to be contaminated by darkness.

Only believe the spoken word.

Declare with me and say:

- Oh God, I command all the cells responsible for health in my body to arise by the power of the Holy Spirit and swallow any stranger in the territory of my body in Jesus Mighty name.

The Presence of God in every Human Body

- I command every attacked cell in my body and mind, and I declare you cannot die, and you are getting stronger in Jesus Mighty name.
- I declare the reproduction of strong cells in my body and skin in Jesus Mighty name.
- Cells of beauty, you cannot be eaten up, I attack every attack in my blood cells in Jesus Mighty name.
- Every inherited sickness in my blood and cells let the power of the Creator arise and swallow you in Jesus Mighty name. I refuse to be comfortable with inherited diseases in my blood and body in Jesus Mighty name.
- I instruct the encoded instructions in my DNA to align with God's creation Agenda for my life. Every corrupted Cell, receive restoration from the Creator in Jesus Mighty name.

Watch and Pray

CHAPTER THREE

WHAT IS A DNA or Deoxyribonucleic Acid? (Branden, 2005)

DNA is a nucleic acid that contains the Genetic instructions used in the development and functioning of all known living Creatures.

THE FUNCTIONS OF A DNA

The main role of DNA molecules is the long-term storage of information

- The DNA segments that carry this genetic information are called Genes.
- The information in the DNA is stored as a code made up of four chemical bases: adenine (A), guanine (G), cytosine (C), and thymine (T). Human DNA consists of about 3 billion bases, and more than 99 percent of those bases are the same in all people.
- DNA bases pair up with each other, A with T and C with G, to form units called base pairs. Each base is also attached to a sugar molecule and a phosphate.

Watch and Pray

- An important property of DNA is that it can replicate, or make copies of itself. Each strand of DNA in the double helix can serve as a pattern for duplicating the sequence of bases. This is critical when cells divide because each new cell needs to have an exact copy of the DNA present in the old cell.

Every one of us is unique. The most incredible thing about genes is that all humans of every race, ethnic group, religion, and gender share 99.9% of the same genes. The remaining 0.1% accounts for all the differences among human beings. Just think of it. There are seven billion plus people on this planet. 99.9% of the human recipe is identical. It is a mere one tenth of a percent of a person's genetic code which makes every single person unlike anyone else.

So how did you receive the genetic coding that makes you unique?

- Each person, inherited their parents' genes. Your parents' sex cells carry the unique genetic blueprint of each parent.
- The Human body cells have 23 pairs of chromosomes, which is a total of 46 chromosomes.
- A child receives 23 chromosomes from the female and 23 from a male to form total of 46 chromosomes required to create a human being. During conception, the genes of both parents are passed down to the next generation.

As you pray in Jesus name, understand that the results of your intercession are surely coming your way. It is confirmed scripturally in John 14:14, where Jesus says, "Ask anything in

WHAT IS A DNA or Deoxyribonucleic Acid?

My name, and I will do it". He is the God who created the DNA; He is the God that knows how your body is held up together. Even when you are weak your body still stands together.

All things are held together in Christ Jesus our Lord

"And he himself is before all things, and in him all things are held together" (Colossians 1:17).

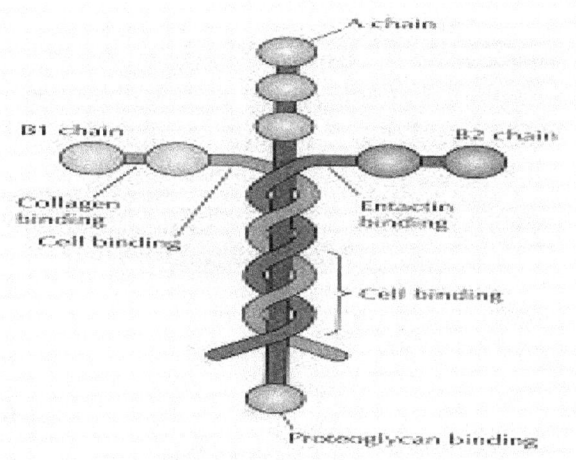

The figure above is a cellular structure that holds our bodies together; what holds our physical body together is cellular proteins consisting of cells in the shape of the cross. To me this structure confirms that the God of the cross is the God that created all flesh. It is not nature, evolution or science that created the earth and mankind. Child of God, continue to fix your eyes on the cross, that is where our salvation comes from. The very same cross, is in you and sustaining the shape of your body.

God's Signature revealed in a human body

I am that I am - That is, "I am what I am". The words express absolute, and therefore, unchanging and eternal being.

Two names God would now be known by. A name that speaks what He is in Himself, I am that I am - This explains his name Jehovah, and signifies,

1. That He is Self-Existent; He has His being of Himself, and has no dependence upon any other. And being Self - Existent He cannot but be self-sufficient, and therefore, all-sufficient, and the inexhaustible fountain of being and ecstasy.

2. That He is Eternal and Unchangeable, always the same, yesterday today, and forever: He will be what He will be, and what He is.

3. That He is Faithful and True to all his promises; and unchangeable in his Word as well as in His nature, and He is not a man that He should lie or change His Mind.

"And God spake unto Moses, and said unto him, I am the LORD (YHVH). And I appeared unto Abraham, unto Isaac, and unto Jacob, by the name of God Almighty, but by my name JEHOVAH was I not known to them" (Exodus 6:2 KJV).

WHAT IS A DNA or Deoxyribonucleic Acid?

"And God said unto Moses I AM THAT I AM: and he said, thus shalt thou say unto the children of Israel, I AM hath sent me unto you" (Exodus 3:14 KJV).

Based upon the revelation from the book of Exodus, the ancient Hebrew name of God YHVH is revealed. This particular name was believed to be so sacred, hold such power, and command such reverence. Traditionally, the name was spoken only by the high priest during temple services, intoning it on the Day of Atonement (utter with particular sound, recite with prolonged sound). Because the name revealed to Moses was originally recorded in biblical Hebrew without the vowels, today we are left with no way of knowing precisely how the name of YHVH was spoken. The majority of scholarly opinion holds that, in the day of Moses, YHVH was pronounced 'Yah-Weigh' in the pronunciation, the letter V is replaced with the sound of the W, although there is no W in the Hebrew alphabet.

In each cell of every life: The God Code is revealed

Genetic research is based on the understanding that all life is formed as combinations of only four chemical compounds. These basic units of life – adenine, thymine, guanine and cystosine (A, T, G and C respectively) - called DNA Bases. They carry all of the information required to produce every form of life that is known to exist. From the smallest single-celled organisms to the estimated 100 trillion cells that make up a single human body; the code of each life form is made from different arrangement of these four bases.

Watch and Pray

The alphabet of DNA: translated

The key to translating the code of DNA into meaningful language is to apply the discovery that converts elements to letters based upon their matching values, hydrogen become the Hebrew letter Yod (Y), nitrogen becomes the letter Hey (H), Oxygen becomes letter Vav (V), and Carbon become letter Gimel (G). These substitutions now reveal that the ancient form of God's name, YH, exists as the literal chemistry of our genetic code. Through this bridge between God's name and the elements of modern science, it now becomes possible to reveal the full mystery and find greater meaning in the ancient code that lives as each cell of our bodies.

The figure below shows the four DNA Bases, showing the elements that they are made of, and equivalent of each element in the Hebrew alphabet. As our genetic code is made of combinations of DNA Bases, sometimes hundreds of letters long, there are a tremendous number of ways that YHVG may be combined in our cells.

WHAT IS A DNA or Deoxyribonucleic Acid?

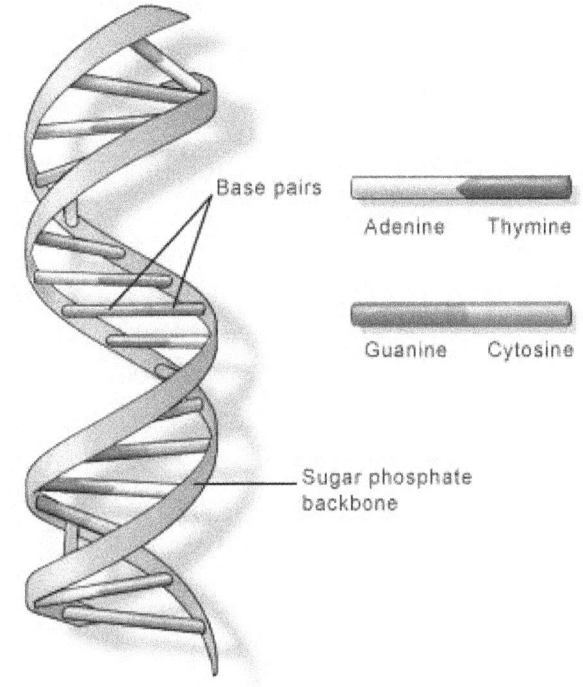

U.S. National Library of Medicine

DNA

If you want to understand the human body, you must be acquainted with deoxyribonucleic acid, or DNA. Without DNA your cells would not produce the proteins you need and would not know what role to play to keep you going.

If you look closely at the strand of DNA above, the first thing you will notice is its special shape. The double-helix structure of DNA reminds us of a twisted ladder. If you look

Watch and Pray

carefully, you will see that this "ladder" is actually two chains of nucleotides bound together.

What is a nucleotide? A nucleotide consists of deoxyribose sugar, a phosphate group, and a set of nitrogen bases. The sugar and the phosphates form the sides of the ladder. The nitrogen bases form the rungs of the ladders. There are four nitrogen bases: adenine (A), thymine (T), cytosine (C), and guanine (G). The bases pair up in specific ways to form the rungs. Adenine always pairs with thymine, and cytosine always pairs with guanine.

DNA BASE	CHEMICAL ELEMENT			HEBREW LETTER	value
Thymine (T)	Hydrogen	=	Yod	Y	10
	Nitrogen	=	Hey	H	5
	Oxygen	=	Vav	V	6
	Carbon	=	Gimel	G	3
Cytosine (C)	Hydrogen		Yod	Y	10
	Nitrogen		Hey	H	5
	Oxygen		Vav	V	6
	Carbon		Gimel	G	3
Adenine	Hydrogen		Yod	Y	10

WHAT IS A DNA or Deoxyribonucleic Acid?

(A)	Nitrogen	Hey	H	5
	Oxygen	Vav	V	6
	Carbon	Gimel	G	3
Guanine (G)	Hydrogen	Yod	Y	10
	Nitrogen	Hey	H	5
	Oxygen	Vav	V	6
	Carbon	Gimel	G	3

Replacing the final H in YHVH with the chemical equivalent of nitrogen, God's name becomes the elements hydrogen, nitrogen, oxygen and nitrogen. (HNON) all colourless, odourless and invisible INET gases. In other words, replacing 100% of God's personal name with the elements of this world creates a substance that is an intangible, yet very real form of creation. We are told of God that He is omnipresence, invisible in nature but visible through manifestation of his work.

God's Name	As Elements		Human kind's Name	As Elements
	Chemical Equivalent			
Y	Hydrogen	=	Y	Hydrogen
H	Nitrogen	=	H	Nitrogen

Watch and Pray

V	Oxygen	=	V	Oxygen
H	nitrogen	-	G	Carbon

The above figure illustrates that the H in the YHVH of God's name is replaced by G in the YHVG of humankind. Through language, this illustrates that while we share the 3 of the 4 letters of God's personal name as our genetic code, we are not equal to God. 25 % of our composition is very different. It is this difference that gives us our physicality and accounts for our uniqueness as human beings. The last letter of our name is what gives us colour, taste, texture and sounds of our body: carbon.

The timeless name of God: YHVH

OUR GOD IS NOT LIMITED BY TIME. YH in the Mankind's DNA which gives us the same character of God and of being Eternal Beings. We can be limited by what we allow, for we are 100 % spirit being residing in the body. Our spirit being cannot be limited by time, since we are eternal beings living in the mortal bodies.

The name God gave to Moses

The word Eternal means, "Existence having no beginning or end and functioning beyond the limitations of time".

We share the never ending quality with our God through 75% of the elements that define our genetic code.

When a baby is conceived, it means eternal life is imparted in the mortal womb by God. If the foetus die in the womb, or

WHAT IS A DNA or Deoxyribonucleic Acid?

is aborted he/she is still an eternal being because it is a spirit. When you are aborted it simply means that your body was denied access to enter the earth realm. Your spirit can never be terminated.

The example above is meant to show us how serious God was when He created men. The creation of men was not a simple worthless arrangement, no wonder when men sinned against God in the Garden of Eden, it angered and disappointed God. For this reason, God could not just eliminate Adam & Eve to end His problems. But He had to provide a redemption plan for mankind. You cannot conceive a child (or impregnate a woman) and because of your present conditions of maybe rape case or, poverty decide to terminate the pregnancy and conclude that your problems are over. My dear sister and brother that child is waiting for you somewhere in the spirit realm. You can terminate the flesh but not the spirit because all spirits are eternal beings. Life is more serious than how we take it. If we can unlock our imagination and read God's Word, master His principles and pray, we can do what He does, for we are God's own creation made in His likeness. Therefore, even when men sin, they must repent to obtain forgiveness. God can forgive any person who recognises his/her sins. Even when they are as red as crimson, they shall be as white as snow. Hallelujah.

"When the Spirit of truth comes, he will guide you into all the truth, for he will not speak on his own authority, but whatever he hears he will speak, and he will declare to you the things that are to come" (John 16:13 NRSV).

YHVH= THE NAME OF GOD

Watch and Pray

YHVG= NAME OF A MAN

YH means: God or Eternal. The first two letters of the original name of God form one-half of God's name and the name is coded into our cells.

"Jesus answered them, "Is it not written in your Law, I said, you are gods?" (John 10:34 NKJV).

"And the LORD said to Moses, "See, I have made you like God to Pharaoh, and your brother Aaron shall be your prophet" (Exodus 7:1 KJV). "He shall speak for you to the people, and he shall be your mouth, and you shall be as God to him" (Exodus 4:16 KJV).

"I said, "You are gods, sons of the Most High, all of you" (Psalm 82:6 KJV).

Note this Again: YH means Eternal or God. This is the first letters of the personal name of God. The very same letters YH are found in the DNA of every man. We are gods. As soon as we familiarize ourselves with this God given identity we can be able to claim the authority and the benefits attached to it.

Jesus's death and resurrection restored us back to Genesis 1:26-28, and made us according to Revelation 1:6.

"So God created man in his own image, in the image of God he created him; male and female he created them. And God blessed them. And God said to them, "Be fruitful and multiply and fill the earth and subdue it and have dominion over the fish of the sea and over the birds of the heavens and over every living thing that moves on the earth" (Genesis 1:27-28 KJV).

"And hath made us kings and priests unto God and his Father; to him be glory and dominion for ever and ever. Amen" (Revelation 1:6 KJV).

WHAT IS A DNA or Deoxyribonucleic Acid?

VG of mankind's name MEANS within the body

YHVG means 'GOD ETERNAL WITHIN THE BODY' (below is the message that is revealed when the chemistry of our cells is translated into letters of ancient Hebrew).

God's presence 'within the body' Thymine, Cytosine, Adenine and Guanine are the combination of hydrogen, nitrogen, oxygen and carbon that make up the DNA bases. As we replace each element with its equivalent Hebrew letter, we are shown precisely how human life is created from variations of God's name in our bodies.

Let us declare and say: Let god's name arise from every cell in my body and scatter every limitation within me in Jesus name. I am a spirit being and my body listens and obeys my declarations in Jesus name. Amen

If a person dies, it is only the body that is buried because the spirit of every person conceived is eternal. The Spirit returns back to the God who gave it.

"I know that, whatsoever God doeth, it shall be for ever: nothing can be put to it, nor anything taken from it: and God doeth it, that men should fear before him" (Ecclesiastes 3:14 KJV).

In conclusion of this matter

God's name is engraved in every cell of our body, how can the name of God be eaten by sicknesses in our cells? I am talking about the name that heals, the name that makes the blind to see, the lame to walk, the deaf to hear, the name that is above all names.

Watch and Pray

As the Patriarchs and Matriarchs encountered God in their walk with Him, they gave Him names and He also introduced Himself with different names. He is a self-sufficient God, He is an inexhaustible God no wonder He has so many names that actually reveal His Character and ability. These names of God are still relevant to men today. If you believe that He is a Man of war, you can be sure of victory in every battle. The table below is a list of some of the names of God as found in scriptures. The intention of including the names of God in this chapter, is to remind you that the name of God is engraved in every cell in your body.

Also, to help you in the process of mind setting or fighting the battles of the mind and life knowing that you are not a grasshopper, loser, poor or useless. When you check God's names, there's nothing like God of the poor or God of the grasshoppers, therefore, you must delete them from the list of your mind regardless of the failure and disappointments you may experience in the way of life. The Bible records that though a righteous man may fall seven times, they will rise again. Many are the afflictions of the righteous, but God delivers him from all of them. When fear comes, remember that He is Jehovah Rohi Your Shepherd. When you are needy and desperate, remember that He is your provider, and He is the God that is always there. Develop a culture and lifestyle of professing faith regardless of what life throws at you. Judge Jehovah faithfully. Do not imagine against the Lord, do not conspire with the enemy against the Lord through the confessions of your mouth.

WHAT IS A DNA or Deoxyribonucleic Acid?

The Names of God as revealed in the Scriptures

THE NAMES OF YAHWEH	THE MEANING	SCRIPTURE REFERENCE
• Jehova Elohim	The eternal creator	Genesis 2:4-25
• Adonai Jehovah	The Lord our master	Genesis 15:2
• Jehovah Jireh	The Lord the provider	Genesis 22:8
• Jehova Nissi	The Lord our banner	Exodus 17:15
• Jehova Ropheka	The Lord our Healer	Exodus 15:26
• Jehova Shalom	The Lord our Peace	Judges 6:24
• Jehovah Tsidkeenu	The Lord our Righteousness	Jeremiah 23:6
• Jehovah Mekaddishkem	The Lord our Sanctifier	Exodus 31:13
• Jehovah Sabaoth	The Lord of Hosts	1 Samuel 1:11
• Jehovah Shammah	The Lord is present	Ezekiel 48:35

Watch and Pray

• Jehovah Elyon	The Lord Most High	Psalm 7:17
• Jehovah Rohi	The Lord is my Shepherd	Psalm 23:1
• Jehovah Hoseenu	The Lord our maker	Psalm 95:6
• Jehovah Eloheenu	The Lord our God	Psalm 99:5
• Jehovah Eloheka	The Lord thy God	Exodus 20:2
• Jehovah Elohay	The Lord my God	Zechariah 14:5
• Jehovah EL-Gibbor	The Mighty God who never loose any battle	Deut 32:29
• Jehovah EL Chai	The living God	Deut 3:24

CHAPTER FOUR

YOU ARE TRUSTED BY GOD

Many times in our prayers, we pray what we do not fully understand. We ask God to use us without understanding the impact of our prayers. Should He agree to use you, will you stand for the assignment? We look at anointed ministers and we desire their anointing, without us thinking and knowing the graves, the valleys, diseases and sacrifices they had to go through before they reached those dimensions of the anointing. God will not use anyone, unless He has first tested them.

The book of John 11 speaks of a certain man named Lazarus of Bethany. He was loved by the Lord. He and His family were friends of the Lord. One day Lazarus fell sick, he thought the situation will be better, and the situation grew worse. Prayer warriors would come to pray all manner of prayers for brother Lazarus and to give him words of hope concerning the situation he was going through. As he grew

Watch and Pray

worse, panic and desperation hit the sisters enough for them to send a messenger to the Lord.

"He whom you love is very sick", they expected their friend and Master to show up in their chronos (time), but He loved him so much that He delayed to arrive when expected. There is something significant about time, one-minute delay can cause irreparable damage. But not with the Lord Jesus. He knew that this whole situation with Lazarus is not unto death, but unto the glory of God. But how can we say the situation is not unto death while actually Lazarus died in the literal sense? He was wrapped with grave clothes; he was absent from his house for four days. His sisters, friends and relatives, mourned for this great man. But Jesus spoke, the situation is not unto death but unto the glory of God.

Facts can change

"Those who trust in the Lord are like Mount Zion which can never be shaken. As the mountain surround Jerusalem, so the Lord surround His people both now and forever" (Psalm 125:1-2 KJV).

Child of God, you are surrounded by Angels of the Living God. The situation might be saying you are in the tomb. The spirit of sickness, death and the grave may be pursuing your life, to a point where it feels like you are losing the battle; allow yourself to lose the battle because you were never in control. The battle is never yours, if you fight it with your own strength you will be drained and eventually lose your connection with the Lord. Sometimes losing the battle humbles us, and in the process victory is given to us without any human help. Can you trust God enough that He will come through for you? Trust

You are Trusted by God

Him, He loves you enough to raise you from the dead, if need be.

Let God give you victory His way, thy will be done in my life.

Many times when we find ourselves under pressure, we pray prayers that attempt to manipulate God to act; we want to put Him in the corner and expect Him to do what we want, and even give us victory the way we have authored and imagined how our victory should be like. That is selfishness, and God does not work according to our desperate prayers. He is moved by our faith, when you pray understand that God is Almighty, He is Mighty enough not to answer our prayers at the time we want answers. He remains God regardless of our existence. God has been God before He thought of creating mankind. Even when we pass away, people and the land do not remember us anymore, He will still be God. Our prayers should change us, they should prepare and position us to receive from Him by Faith. Our prayers will not change God, because God is not made God by our prayers or our existence. Our presence enhances the pleasure for Him to behold the works of His hands and the fulfilment He gets for answering our prayers.

Last Miracle before the Cross

It was necessary for Lazarus to die, so that His resurrection can glorify the Son of God and cause many to believe in Him. The death of Lazarus was necessary to establish and usher in the Kingdom of God on earth. There is something different and special about the death of Lazarus. The man Lazarus was

Watch and Pray

not the first person to die and be resurrected by our Lord Jesus. There were two other people that Jesus resurrected but they never made it to the grave, Jarius's daughter and the widow's only son. But Lazarus was the first man who was not only declared dead, but was buried. In three to five days, his body started decomposing. According to science, it is proven that it is impossible for a decomposed matter to return to life. The voice of Jesus commanded every decomposed part of Lazarus body to receive life. His decomposed veins, tissues, fibres and all productive organs came back to life. That is the power of Jesus Christ, the Word that became flesh. When the Word of God is spoken, it echoes through dead situations and commands life and life must comply and manifest.

From the grave to the table

Many of us would expect a dead man to rise and go to the hospital in Intensive care unit, because he was terminally ill when he died, but Lazarus rose to dine with Jesus at the table. You can understand that Jesus did not only resurrect Lazarus but he also healed him. People travelled from different parts of the country to come and see not only Jesus, but he who was dead and now alive. Many believed in Jesus, but this particular miracle caused many to believe and it also ushered Jesus to the cross with so much honour and glory. Even after Jesus's death, Lazarus continued to be a constant reminder of the Kingdom Power that Jesus introduced and a testimony of the great work of the Kingdom.

You are Trusted by God

Jesus raises the widow's son at Nain

Soon afterwards he went to a town called Nain, and his disciples and a large crowd went with him. As he approached the gate of the town, a man who had died was being carried out. He was his mother's only son, and she was a widow; and with her was a large crowd from the town. When the Lord saw her, He had compassion for her and said to her, "Do not weep." Then He came forward and touched the bier, and the bearers stood still. And he said, "Young man, I say to you, rise!" The dead man sat up and began to speak, and Jesus gave him to his mother. Fear seized all of them; and they glorified God, saying, "A great prophet has risen among us!" and "God has looked favourably on his people! "This word about him spread throughout Judea and all the surrounding country" (Read Luke 7:11-17 ESV).

Jairus' daughter and a woman with chronic bleeding

"Jesus again crossed to the other side of the Sea of Galilee in a boat. A large crowd gathered around him by the seashore. A synagogue leader named Jairus also arrived. When he saw Jesus, he quickly bowed down in front of him. He begged Jesus, "My little daughter is dying. Come, lay your hands on her so that she may get well and live." Jesus went with the man. A huge crowd followed Jesus and pressed him on every side" (Mark 5:21-24 GW).

"While Jesus was still speaking to her, some people came from the synagogue leader's home. They told the synagogue leader, "Your daughter has died. Why bother the teacher anymore?" When Jesus overheard what they said, he told the synagogue leader, "Don't be afraid! Just believe." (Mark 5:35-36 GW)

From the case studies we went through above, we understand the power of Faith and the spoken Word. There are similarities from the Lazarus

Watch and Pray

story and Jarius's daughter. Jesus said to His disciples; Lazarus sickness is not unto death but unto the Glory of God. This statement on its own tell us that Lazarus death was not personal but about God. Jehovah had to be glorified and Lazarus life was the chosen one to manifest that glory. Sickness and death were used as instruments to manifest the glory. The devil meant to hurt Lazarus and his family, but God knew all along what a way of escape would be for Lazarus. And how many people will come to believe in Jesus through Lazarus death.

With Jarius's daughter, her healing was hijacked by the woman with the issue of blood that was occupying the woman's life for twelve years. And Jarius's daughter was also twelve years of age. We can assume that when the girl was born the woman with the issue of blood began to be sick. And when the daughter turned twelve years she began to be so sick and the spirit of death began to pursue her life. On the twelfth year, the woman with the issue of blood was contemplating and working on her faith to receive her miracle. The miracle that was packaged for the girl was taken by the woman. When the transfer from the hem of the garment of Jesus to the woman with the issue of blood took place, Jarius' daughter died. The only thing that could bring her back was Jarius' belief. Jesus said to Jarius', when you are an assigned vessel that must bring honour to the Father on matters that are pertaining to the Kingdom, what will sustain you is to only Believe. Believe that God loves you so much to make decisions that will work for your good. Don't look at logic, only believe, don't look at the facts, only believe. Don't listen to people that plant fear and worry, only believe! Jesus came to Jarius house and commanded the girl and said:"Talitha koum!" which means 'little girl, I say to you, arise". Jarius' daughter rose to life and both the woman with the issue of blood and Jarius' won. With Jehovah EL - Gibbor, we are guaranteed a win-win outcome, you will never lose any battle, just find grace to endure the process! Amen.

CHAPTER FIVE

NEBUCADNEZZAR YOU ARE FLESH, YOUR WORD IS NOT THE FINAL AUTHORITY

"Then the herald loudly proclaimed, "Nations and peoples of every language, this is what you are commanded to do: As soon as you hear the sound of the horn, flute, zither, lyre, harp, pipe and all kinds of music, you must fall down and worship the image of gold that King Nebuchadnezzar has set up. Whoever does not fall down and worship will immediately be thrown into a blazing furnace" (Daniel 3:4-6 NIV)

There is a battle raging over our worship to the living God. It's a longstanding battle, heating up as we see the forces of darkness aligning in greater measure. Daniel 3 gives us a picture of how our worship to God infuriates the kingdom of darkness. We see the manifestation of this anger against the church in the kingdoms of this world.

Nebuchadnezzar commanded everyone, everywhere in high and low regard to bow down and worship the golden image when they would hear the sound of the musical instruments being played.

Watch and Pray

The strategy of the enemy is at all costs to get us to look away from the Lord and look to the reality of our situations, and be ensnared in the loud sound of pain.

Shadrach, Meshach, and Abednego refused to worship any god but the living God. When they first arrived in Babylon, they had purposed along with Daniel not to defile themselves with the royal food and wine. After following their diet for ten days, they were healthier and better nourished than any of the young men who ate the royal food. Daniel 1: 20 says, "In every matter of wisdom and understanding about which the king questioned them, he found them ten times better than all the magicians and enchanters in his entire kingdom."

Not even the threat of death converted them. When found in death threatening situation, many people reconsider their stance. Child of God, remember physical death is not your ultimate destiny. You will die one day anyway. Our choices and decisions mustn't be influenced by threat directed at us. Let your Yes be Yes and your No be No. So, their refusal to worship the golden image that King Nebuchadnezzar set up infuriated him, and he had the furnace heated seven times hotter than normal. The furnace was so hot that the flames of the fire killed the soldiers preparing to throw the men in. You may be walking through a fiery situation that the enemy has heated seven times hotter than normal, at times you may find yourself in multiple fiery situations but guess who is with you in the fire; The Lord of Hosts is ever present!

Nebucadnezzar you are Flesh, your Word in not the Final Authority

Confidence in God is faith in action

The God we serve is able to deliver us, from the enemy and from his fire, and from the world system. Even if He does not come, that would not mean that He is not able. It simply means He is ALL Powerful and ALL knowing enough that He can choose how to deliver and when to deliver His own.

"If we are thrown into the blazing furnace, the God we serve is able to deliver us from it, and he will deliver us from Your Majesty's hand. But even if he does not, we want you to know, Your Majesty, that we will not serve your gods or worship the image of gold you have set up. Then Nebuchadnezzar was furious with Shadrach, Meshach and Abednego, and his attitude toward them changed. He ordered the furnace heated seven times hotter than usual and commanded some of the strongest soldiers in his army to tie up Shadrach, Meshach and Abednego and throw them into the blazing furnace. Then these men were bound in their cloaks, their tunics, their hats, and their other garments, and they were thrown into the burning fiery furnace. The king's command was so urgent and the furnace so hot that the flames of the fire killed the soldiers who took up Shadrach, Meshach and Abednego, So Shadrach, Meshach, and Abednego, securely tied, fell into the roaring flames. But suddenly, Nebuchadnezzar jumped up in amazement and exclaimed to his advisers, "Didn't we tie up three men and throw them into the furnace?" "Yes, Your Majesty, we certainly did," they replied. He answered and said, Behold, I see four men loose, walking in the midst of the fire, and they have no hurt; and the form of the fourth is like the Son of God" (Daniel 3: 17 -18 NIV).

Watch and Pray

Your enemies see the Son of God

It was Nebuchadnezzar who saw the fourth man, who looked like the son of God walking around in the midst of the fire. The Hebrew number for four is Dalet, it means a door. Jesus is the Door, the way to our deliverance. We may not always perceive the Lord in the midst of a trial, but be assured that Satan sees the Lord by your side. For He will never leave you or forsake you! The men emerged from an impossible situation unbound, unharmed, and were accelerated to their place of prominence.

You are emerging strong from every battle you are facing. He said to Joshua, as I was with Moses, I will be with you. As you fight, fight strong knowing I am directing your sword, I am directing the stone right to Goliath's forehead. The enemy's conversion is in seeing but your Faith should be on things not seen. Trust God even if you can't trace Him, trust His Word, for He has exalted His Word above all His name. He is a good God that provides the oxygen free of charge even to those who hate Him and chose not to worship Him. So when He judge, He is Justified!

CHAPTER SIX

REJECTED AND FALLEN

"Now there was a man of Benjamin, whose name was Kish, the son of Abiel, the son of Zeror, the son of Bechorath, the son of Aphiah, a Benjamite, a mighty man of power. And he had a son, whose name was Saul, a choice young man, a goodly: and there was not among the children of Israel a goodlier person than he: from his shoulders and upward he was higher than any of the people" (1 Samuel 9:1-3 KJV).

God's Anointing

When Israel cried for a king, God picked this handsome, goodly man to be captain over his inheritance Israel. Saul was an answer to the prayer and to the cry of the people. Prophet Samuel was instructed by God to anoint Saul, not because Saul prayed for the position, but because the people cried for a King and God in His faithfulness He responded by qualifying Saul to become the first King, taking over the reins from King Yahweh himself.

Over the years we see God being King over Israel and this is what made Israel different from other nations; but as Israel got exposed to the world system the people began to cry for uniformity with their neighbours.

Test of trust and trustworthiness

Saul as the sovereign King of Israel, God began to trust him with His battles. And God began to speak to Samuel about the outstanding battle against the enemies of God and of Israel which King Saul must deal with. Through Prophet Samuel, God instructs King Saul concerning Amalek, the greatest enemy of Israel. God was testing the obedience of King Saul and his trustworthiness.

The test was not different from Abraham's test, when God said to him: Take now your son, your only son, Isaac, whom you love, go to the land of Moriah, and offer him there as a burnt offering upon one of the mountains I will tell you of. You see God's tests are not written Test one (1) or two (2) or three (3). They usually come as situations that appear at home, work, church, market place, where God tests obedience and character. You later realise, there has always been a force beyond yourself, and there were discussions in heaven and God orchestrated the situation to see our attitude and obedience, moreover to reveal to us our true nature. When the enemy tempts us in order to steal, kill and destroy us, God on the other hand uses the same situation to test and prepare us for promotion. It is always a double sided case. There is the enemy's version and there is God's version of the report concerning our destiny; but which report do we believe?

Saul's insubordination towards God's direct instructions has caused him and his descendants the throne, the position,

Rejected and Fallen

and the power. Saul gave up his children's spiritual inheritance to Agag like Adam to Satan. Saul's descendants were cut off from taking over as Kings after him. They were demoted from prince's status to subjects.

Who is Agag?

Agag was a dynastic name of the kings of Amalek, just as Pharaoh was used as a dynastic name for the ancient Egyptian Kings.

Who is Amalek?

Amalek is the name of the grandson of Esau, his descendants were called Amalekites.

Who was Saul?

The children of Israel demanded for a king like the nations of the world were having kings.

Now Prophet Samuel took a flask of oil and poured it on the head of Saul and kissed him and said: Has not the Lord anointed you to be captain over His people Israel? So Saul was actually the first King of the kingdom of Israel descending from the smallest tribe of Benjamin the son of Jacob. (See 1 Samuel 10).

"And Samuel said unto Saul, The LORD sent me to anoint thee to be king over his people, over Israel: now, therefore, hearken thou unto the voice of the words of the LORD" (1 Samuel 15:1 JUB).

Watch and Pray

What was God's instruction to King Saul?

"Thus saith the Lord of hosts, I remember that which Amalek did to Israel, how he laid wait for him in the way, when he came up from Egypt. Now go and smite Amalek, and utterly destroy all that they have, and spare them not, but slay both man and women, infant and suckling, ox and sheep, camel and ass" (1 Samuel 15:2-3 JUB).

Partial obedience is disobedience

Saul indeed gathered the people together, and numbered them in Telaim, two hundred thousand footmen, and ten thousand men of Judah.

"And Saul smote and defeated Amalek from Havilah as far as Shur that is over against Egypt. And he took Agag, the king of the Amalekites, alive and utterly destroyed all the people with the edge of the sword. But Saul and the people spared Agag and the best of the sheep and of the oxen and of the fatlings and the lambs and all that was good and would not utterly destroy them, but everything that was vile and refuse, that they destroyed utterly" (1 Samuel 15: 7-9 JUB).

What was King Saul's Transgression?

The instructions to King Saul were very clear. God actually said to King Saul, you were not there when your forefathers came out of Egypt, but I was there. You cannot remember what happened because you were told what happened, but I do remember. I witnessed it. When Israel was weak and faint, on the way to purpose, she needed help, she was thirsty, she needed support, but his brother Esau lay wait and attacked her from behind. When she least expected, she could not even defend herself. Esau and his descendant Amalek were cruel to

Rejected and Fallen

Israel and showed no mercy when Israel needed it the most. It was the Almighty that was dealing with Israel but Amalek wanted no peace and he offended me. God was simply saying this battle is mine, you are partnering with me to finish what is been long overdue. Victory is sure, just listen and do as I tell you. Do as you see me do, do as you hear me say.

Listening is a Skill

> "Delayed obedience is disobedience"
> "Partial obedience is disobedience"

- Firstly, God instructed Saul to listen to Him.
- Secondly, God expressed His remembrance of what Amalek did to His people.
- Thirdly, God instructed Saul to go smite Amalek and utterly destroy them:
  - All that they have, spare *them* not
  - Slay men, women, infants and suckling (all people)
  - Ox and sheep, camel and ass

The return from a great slaughter

King Saul was very impressed with himself and very confident that all went well.

"And Samuel came to Saul, and Saul said unto him, Blessed be thou of the LORD; I have performed the commandment of the LORD. Then Samuel said, what means then this bleating of the sheep in my ears and

Watch and Pray

the lowing of the oxen which I hear? And Saul said, 'They have brought them from Amalek, for the people spared the best of the sheep and of the oxen to sacrifice unto the LORD thy God, and the rest we have utterly destroyed'" (1 Samuel 13 -15 JUB).

The heart of God

"Be quiet," Samuel told Saul, "and let me tell you what the Lord told me last night." (1 Samuel 15:16 GW).

"Speak," Saul replied.

"Samuel said, 'Even though you don't consider yourself great, you were the head of Israel's tribes. The Lord anointed you king of Israel. And the Lord sent you on a mission. He said, 'Claim those sinners, the Amalekites, for me by destroying them. Wage war against them until they're wiped out.' Why didn't you obey the Lord? Why have you taken their belongings and done what the Lord considers evil?" (1 Samuel 15:17-19 GW).

> "Delayed obedience is disobedience"
> "Partial obedience is disobedience"

Defensive attitude versus repentance

"But I did obey the Lord," Saul told Samuel. "I went where the Lord sent me, brought back King Agag of Amalek, and claimed the Amalekites for God. The army took some of their belongings—the best sheep and cows were claimed for God—in order to sacrifice to the Lord your God in Gilgal." And Samuel said, 'Does the LORD have as great

Rejected and Fallen

delight in burnt offerings and sacrifices as in hearing the voice of the LORD?' Behold, to obey is better than sacrifice and to heed is better than the fat of rams. For rebellion is as (serious as) the sin of witchcraft, and to break the word (disobedience) of the Lord is (as serious as) iniquity and idolatry (false religion). Because thou hast rejected the word of the LORD, he has also rejected you from being king" (1 Samuel 15:20-23 GW).

Pride comes before the fall

"Then Saul said unto Samuel, I have sinned; for I have transgressed the commandment of the LORD and thy words because I feared the people and consented unto their voice. And Samuel said unto Saul, I will not return with thee, for thou hast rejected the word of the LORD, and the LORD has rejected thee from being king over Israel" (1 Samuel 15:24, 26 GW).

The Kingdom is transferred

And as Samuel turned about to go away, Saul laid hold upon the skirt of Samuel's mantle, and it rent. And Samuel said unto him, The LORD has rent the kingdom of Israel from thee today and has given it to a neighbour of thine that is better than thou.

Samuel kills Agag

Saul failed to carry the mandate to the end – He lacked the finishing anointing.

"Samuel finished what Saul was supposed to start with. "And also the Overcomer of Israel will not lie nor repent concerning this, for he is not a man, that he should repent. Then Samuel said, Bring me Agag, the king

Watch and Pray

of Amalek. And Agag came unto him delicately. And Agag said, Surely the bitterness of death is near. And Samuel said, as thy sword has made women childless, so shall thy mother be childless among women. Then Samuel hewed Agag in pieces before the LORD in Gilgal" (1 Samuel 15:29, 32-33 ASV).

The Repercussion of disobedience

The damage, however, was already done. In that one night, the sages teach us, Agag had intercourse with a maidservant who later, gave birth to a son. Thus, over centuries later the Jews were faced with mortal danger from Haman the Agagite.

It is interesting to note that just as Haman is a direct descendant of Agag, both Mordecai and Esther are descendants of Saul. Mordecai is the son of Jair of the tribe of Benjamin. Revenge and attacks knows where to go... many times we wonder, why me?

Whose descendant are you? Do you have records of your forefathers and the battles they left unsettled?

> Everything that happens in our lives happened in the spirit first, your birth, everything has its start and purpose. Whether we understand it or not...
>
> The spirit world dominates the natural world.

Modercai is a descendent from the tribe of Benjamin, who is the son of Jacob; and gave birth to then Kish to Saul, and Saul to Jonathan, who gave birth to Mephibosheth, then Jair gave birth to Mordecai the Jew.

Rejected and Fallen

Why Mephibosheth had to survive – Purpose

Now we see why Mephibosheth had to survive that war, even in his disability he needed to survive so he can provide the seed to fight the seed of Agag the Amalekite that King Saul through his disobedience left behind centuries earlier. *(See 2 Samuel 4:4)*

This war between Haman and Mordercai the Jew, brings us to the celebration of Purim. That is why during Purim the Jews listen to the Torah reading of Deutoronomy 25:17-20. Do not forget what Amalek did to you, Mordecai refused to bow to Haman the Agagite, he knew the plan of God concerning the Amalekite.

Why Vashti had to disobey instructions – be dethroned (Why Esther had to look beautiful – take over the position of the Queen)

Now we see why Queen Vashti had to disobey the voice of her husband, King Ahasuerus. Even if she tried to pretend and do what the king wanted, she would have still been rejected because her term of office was over in the realm of the spirit; therefore, it was necessary for Esther to occupy the office of the Queen. The manifestation of the spirit world was inevitable for both Vashti the Queen and Esther. Her position expired the day Esther came to town, equally so, for King Herod upon the birth of Jesus Christ. There are some people whose position expires upon the birth of others. The great grandfather to Esther, King Saul failed to carry the directive, so it will take somebody in the position of Royalty to undo what he had done. That is why she had to be queen, it was a predestined role.

Watch and Pray

Everything that happens in our lives happened in the spirit first, and they are all purpose driven. Your birth, your beauty, your expulsion from work, everything has a purpose. Whether we understand it or not, sometimes we wonder why was I born in the family that I am born in; why did you marry the woman or man you have married? Could it be that there are battles linked to your blood line that were left undone and only you can win them? Could it be, God needed a seed with your DNA plus the seed of this man who impregnated you, for a divine reason that is not revealed to you? We will never know until we start to enquire of the Lord about everything that happens in our lives, even our decisions, our anger, our bitterness and even our marriages, long before choosing partners.

If you do not wipe out what needs to be wiped out, you will certainly be the one to be wiped out.

Make your choice! The enemy is merciless and your unnecessary mercy will cost you your life, your peace, your wealth, unless you are prepared to go all out for what is yours. Saul showed mercy to King Agag. Here is a million Rand question:

Did Haman show any mercy to Mordecai and the Jews? Can you blame God for Deuteronomy 25:17-19?

Haman's Plot against the Jews

"Later, King Xerxes promoted Haman. (Haman was the son of Hammedatha and was from Agag.) He gave Haman a position higher in authority than all the other officials who were with him. All the king's advisers were at the king's gate, kneeling and bowing to Haman with their faces touching the ground, because the king had commanded it. But

Rejected and Fallen

Mordecai would not kneel and bow to him. Then the king's advisers at the king's gate asked Mordecai, "Why do you ignore the king's command?" Although they asked him day after day, he paid no attention to them. So they informed Haman to see if Mordecai's actions would be tolerated, since Mordecai had told them that he was a Jew. When Haman saw that Mordecai did not kneel and bow to him, Haman was infuriated. Because the king's advisers had informed him about Mordecai's nationality, he thought it beneath himself to kill only Mordecai. So Haman planned to wipe out Mordecai's people—all the Jews in the entire kingdom of Xerxes. In Xerxes' twelfth year as king, Pur (which means the lot) was thrown in front of Haman for every day of every month, from Nisan, the first month, until Adar, the twelfth month. Now, Haman told King Xerxes, "Your Majesty, there is a certain nationality scattered among—but separate from—the nationalities in all the provinces of your kingdom. Their laws differ from those of all other nationalities. They do not obey your decrees. So it is not in your interest to tolerate them, Your Majesty. If you approve, have the orders for their destruction be written. For this I will pay 750,000 pounds of silver to your treasurers to be put in your treasury." At that, the king removed his signet ring and gave it to Haman, the enemy of the Jews. (Haman was the son of Hammedatha and was from Agag.) The king told Haman, "You can keep your silver and do with the people whatever you like" (Esther 3: 1-11 GW)

Haman Prepares to exterminate the Jews

"On the thirteenth day of the first month the king's scribes were summoned. All Haman's orders were written to the king's satraps, the governors of every province, and the officials of every people. They wrote to each province in its own script and to the people in each province in their own language. The orders were signed in the name of King Xerxes and sealed with the king's ring. Messengers were sent with official documents

Watch and Pray

to all the king's provinces. The people were ordered to wipe out, kill, and destroy all the Jews—young and old, women and children—on a single day, the thirteenth day of the twelfth month, the month of Adar. Their possessions were also to be seized. A copy of the document was made public in a decree to every province. All the people were to be ready for this day. The messengers hurried out as the king told them. The decree was also issued at the fortress of Susa. So the king and Haman sat down to drink a toast, but the city of Susa was in turmoil." (Esther 3: 12-15 GW)

Can a community of people be killed because one man refused to bow? The scripture above reveals an enemy greater than Haman. When the enemy can get an opportunity to kill you, he will not hesitate. The decree includes exterminating small children; the enemy knows that out of every child, he sees a man of war against him tomorrow. His plan was to kill the present and the future Jewish nation.

Many wars that the world is faced with today, originate from domestic and household issues. Observe the enemies of Israel; they are not strangers, in actual fact, they are brothers. Other people are blaming Jacob for faking to be Esau, and they see him as a thief. At the same time, we must not forget that Esau sold his birth right. He did not assess and evaluate the value of the birth right; he took for granted what was given to him naturally.

On that very same breath, we must not forget the Author of purpose, who spoke to the mother of the twins and said, *"Two nations are in your womb, and the elder shall serve the younger"*. One way or the other, the scripture must be fulfilled, absolutely everything that God spoke must be fulfilled. Esau and his descendants were predestined to serve Jacob, keeping the birth

Rejected and Fallen

right would have not changed destiny, by selling the birth right for a bowl of soup he was helping destiny to come to pass.

SECTION B:

THE POWER OF THE WORD

CHAPTER SEVEN

SPIRITUAL REVOLUTION

What is a Revolution?

According to Oxford dictionary, a revolution is a forcible overthrow of established government or social order, or political system in favour of a new system. (Emphasis)

A rebellious system led by Nimrod (See Genesis 10:8-12)

After the flood, the sons of Noah had many descendants and dwelled in the land with their fathers. Amongst, the descendants of Noah, there was his great grandson named Nimrod, a grandson of Ham and the sixth son of Cush, identified as a Cushite black. He was a "mighty hunter" before the Lord and a first to establish kingdoms in Babylon, Erech, Akkad, and Calneh in Shinar.

Because God multiplied the descendants of Noah, they were many upon the earth, and they spoke the same language. God expected them to scatter and occupy the whole earth. But under the leadership of Nimrod he influenced the people to gather and live in one place. Moreover, that they should make bricks and burn them thoroughly and not use stones to build

Watch and Pray

their desired tower. They also used slime to build instead of mortar. The people's intention of building the tower was to make a name for themselves and visit heaven.

We learn from the story in Genesis 11 that Nimrod was an influential leader of his people and a rebellious leader against God. Let me qualify my statement by quoting from scripture.

"Now the whole earth spoke one language and used the same words. And as people journeyed eastward, they found a plain in the land of Shinar and they settled there. They said one to another, "Come, let us make bricks and fire them thoroughly [in a kiln, to harden and strengthen them]." So they used brick for stone [as building material], and they used tar (bitumen, asphalt) for mortar. They said, "Come, let us build a city for ourselves, and a tower whose top will reach into the heavens, and let us make a [famous] name for ourselves, so that we will not be scattered [into separate groups] and be dispersed over the surface of the entire earth [as the Lord instructed]." Now the Lord came down to see the city and the tower which the sons of men had built. And the Lord said, "Behold, they are one [unified] people, and they all have the same language. This is only the beginning of what they will do [in rebellion against Me], and now no evil thing they imagine they can do will be impossible for them. Come, let Us (Father, Son, Holy Spirit) go down and there confuse and mix up their language, so that they will not understand one another's speech." So the Lord scattered them abroad from there over the surface of the entire earth; and they stopped building the city. Therefore the name of the city was Babel – because there the Lord confused the language of the entire earth; and from that place the Lord scattered and dispersed them over the surface of all the earth. (Genesis 11: 1-10 AMP).

Spiritual Revolution

Abrahamic system – the God system

After the fall of man, the world and mankind needed reconciliation with the creator to break and reverse the system that the fall ushered in. For the reconciliation agenda to be realized, God had a system in mind to replace and dominate the systems of the world. For God to achieve the dominion mandate of Genesis 1:26, He needed a man who would respond to the call of establishing the system for the kingdom of God.

The sacrificial response of Abram to establish a new order.

Abram's journey begins with instruction and separation

"Now the LORD had said unto Abram, Get thee out of thy country, and from thy kindred, and from thy father's house, unto a land that I will shew thee" (Genesis 12:1 KJV)

The journey of Abram to Abraham started with instructions. When Abram left his country and his relatives, he did not know where he was going. He trusted the God who called him out. Abram departed with a promise to the land he did not know. For Abram to fulfil the assignment before him, it was necessary for him to be separated from his past, from the gods of the land and of his fathers; he needed to separate himself from any potential contamination.

"And I will make of thee a great nation, and I will bless thee, and make thy name great; and thou shalt be a blessing. And I will bless them that bless thee, and curse him that curseth thee: and in thee shall all families of the earth be blessed" (Genesis 12:2-3 KJV).

Watch and Pray

The purpose of God's call for Abram was for the establishment of nations, and it carried an eternal significance. As much as the call of Abram was for God to establish a nation of Israel, but God's purpose was and still is bigger than a nation. God had other nations at heart when He called Abram out. God needed one nation to become a God over, to love and protect, to be King over them and to show other nations how He will deal with them also should they choose to allow Him to be their God and King. Abram's response to the call of God was the birth and beginning of the new order of the Kingdom of God. You can see the weight of a person's call by the tests, challenges, afflictions and delays that a righteous man goes through before the full manifestation of their destiny. I believe that Abram himself did not fully understand what was going on, for the plan was not fully revealed to him, like you and I are today. We have the promise, we have the blood of Jesus, we have the name of Jesus, we have the Holy Spirit, and we have the Word, yet we do not fully understand God's processes of taking us to our place of prominence. At times, we do not even know where He is taking us. What is important in every season, is to hold on to the end results He has shown you, or the Word He has given you have to be trusted enough to know that He knows what He is doing, for He has predestined everything concerning us before He laid the foundations of the earth. We need to be persuaded in our understanding that He is in control regardless of the disappointments, discouragements and delays we tend to experience in our daily lives. We need to elevate our faith to believe with God and like God. When God called Abram He believed in him, when God calls a man He believes in him.

Spiritual Revolution

When God said to Jeremiah, before I formed you in the belly I knew you, and before you came out of the womb I sanctified you, and I ordained you a prophet unto nations. And Jeremiah did not believe in himself, he said to the Lord, I cannot speak: for I am a child. Because God believed in Jeremiah, He said unto him, say not, I am a child: for you Jeremiah shalt go to all that I shall send you, and I have set you over kingdoms, to root out, and to pull down, and to destroy, and to throw down, to build and to plant. Never doubt yourself, the calling of God over your life is an enabler, He ordained success over your life and destiny before you were conceived in your mother's womb. His knowledge of us is too deep. Be not afraid of your enemy's faces, do not be afraid of your problem's face, face it! Every problem has a face, every enemy has a face, when they surface, face them, you are ordained to face them and conquer for the knowledge of their faces are already exposed at your ordination service. (See Jeremiah 1:5).

If Yahweh did not withhold His only begotten son, but gave Him up for us, how can He then not give us all things?

"So Abram departed, as the LORD had spoken unto him; and Lot went with him: and Abram was seventy and five years old when he departed out of Haran. And Abram took Sarai his wife, and Lot his brother's son, and all their substance that they had gathered, and the souls that they had gotten in Haran; and they went forth to go into the land of Canaan; and into the land of Canaan they came" (Genesis 12:4-5 ASV).

Abraham obeyed God and departed from his comfort zone, he departed from his familiar surroundings with his wife and his brother's son Lot to the place where God was leading him. God called Abram alone. The only person he was obligated to take along with, was Sarai, his wife because of marital covenant. As for Lot, was not part of the assignment. Many times we have people who follow us or people we take with to our promise land, yet they do not pursue the same interests as we do. Even when trouble befalls them they still become our responsibility and as a result, we fight their battles because we agreed to take them along. And God remains faithful even in problems we put ourselves in to take us out unharmed and victorious to preserve the purpose in us.

God's system revealed in Abram

It came to pass after the separation of Abram and Lot that He heard that his nephew Lot, was taken in the battle of the nine kings, he armed his 318 trained servants, born in his house, and pursued the enemy to Dan. Abram's agenda was to deliver his nephew from his enemies and recover all his possessions. But God had planned an encounter with Abram after his victory over the nine kings. Sometimes we seem to be just helping our families while we are actually manifesting and fulfilling the purpose of God for our lives.

And they took Lot, Abram's brother's son, who dwelt in Sodom, and his goods, and departed.

"And there came one that had escaped, and told Abram the Hebrew; for he dwelt in the plain of Mamre the Amorite, brother of Eshcol, and brother of Aner: and these were confederate with Abram" (Genesis 14:13 KJV).

Spiritual Revolution

"And when Abram heard that his brother was taken captive, he armed his trained servants, born in his own house, three hundred and eighteen, and pursued them unto Dan. And he divided himself against them, he and his servants, by night, and smote them, and pursued them unto Hobah, which is on the left hand of Damascus. And he brought back all the goods, and also brought again his brother Lot, and his goods, and the women also, and the people" (Genesis 14:12-16 KJV).

- **Abram had military wisdom** – He marshalled an army to fight and defeat the enemy. Abram was not fighting few people; it was nine kingdoms at war, four against five kings. Abram found himself in the midst of the battle of kings and kingdoms because of his nephew that was taken by Chedorlaomer and his acquaintances. The children of God must never relinquish their urge to fight victoriously for what is theirs. If what is yours is taken from you, gird yourself for war. The mission and goal must be clear, the power, the anointing, the grace, the protection, you already have, marshal your army to victory. The Lord is saying to you, go in the strength you have, and rescue your Israel from the hands of the Medianites. I am sending you, saith the Lord (See Judges 6:14). We must not forget that the battle goes on in the realm of the spirit, whether we feel it or not. We will see the manifestation of the outcomes of the warfare in our natural lives.

Watch and Pray

> Do not forget, the battle goes on,
> "whether you feel it or not"

- **Abram was a strategist** - Abram divided his forces against them *by night*, and he and his servants attacked and pursued them as far as Hobah, which is north of Damascus. Victorious people understand the times and seasons. *Most battles are better fought in the night* when the enemy has poor vision. We must keep watch at midnight and know it is time for warfare and victory. Abram had the secret of the night, hence, he organized his army to attack by night. The book of Exodus records the events that took place a night before departure from Egypt. At midnight the angel of death passed through Egypt, and all the first born of the Egyptians died, both man and beast. I believe that Jehovah Saboath is still fighting for His people at midnight. There is a secret about the night watch that we need to pursue and tap into so we can be progressive and conquer the enemy against our lives.
- **Fight to win** – when Abram heard that someone who belonged to him was taken, he arose. Many times when something from us is taken, we feel paralyzed, but Abram arose. We receive the same tenacious grace as Abram today. And the mission and his goal for this battle were clear to him and his men; to rescue Lot, and everything and everyone that belong to him. Abram did not focus on how big the armies of the enemy were, but

Spiritual Revolution

he focused on rescuing Lot. He knew, he had a promise, therefore, *becoming a casualty in battle and dying in the process was not an option for Abram*. Be conscious of the promise upon your life, in trying moments, the promise and the calling will keep you alive in battle. Judah, the great grandson of Abram was still in his loins, Kings were still in his loins, how can he then die in battle? There are nations waiting for you and I to manifest, there are nations waiting to hear your voice, how can we then die in battle? There are captives in your family and community waiting for you to minister salvation and deliverance, how can you die in battle? There is a problem in society and in business waiting for you to bring a multibillion solution, how can you die in battle? Yes, diseases will attack nations, chaos will break out, crisis situations will come upon men, man-made viruses and wars will break forth to advance the kingdom of darkness, but, it will not come near your dwelling. Darkness and light cannot share the same space. And dying before fulfilling your purpose is not an option. Therefore, arise and face the enemy in prayer and act as the Holy Spirit reveals and instruct you. Victory is yours. Hallelujah.

The bible records that the King of Sodom, the king of Gomorrah, the king of Admah the king of Zeboiim and the king of Bela went out and joined in battle with them in the valley of Siddim, that is Chedorlomer, the king of Elam, Tidal king of the Gentiles, Amraphel king of Shinar and Arioch king of Ellasar. That was four kings against five.

Watch and Pray

The valley was full of slime pits and the king of Sodom and Gomorrah fled and fell there; and those that remained fled to the mountain. And they took all the goods of Sodom and Gomorrah and all their provisions and went away. And they also took Lot, Abram's brother's son, who dwelt in Sodom, and his goods and departed.

Can I talk to somebody who has lost something in life? The enemy took all the goods of Sodom and Gomorrah, not only that, they took all their provisions. On top of all the goods and provisions, they took Lot, Abram's nephew also to captivity. Abram girded himself for battle, his army with him. And God honoured his faith and supported his move. His resources were not as enough as compared to the nine kings. But he defeated the armies that looked stronger than his. He knew that there is a higher power behind him. The higher power that called him out; the higher power that revealed the destiny of his descendants before his son Isaac was conceived. He believed, therefore, he acted, as a result, Lot was rescued; everything was restored to him, and he got even the spoils from the enemy properties. Abram gave tithes of all the spoils to Melchizedek the priest of the Most High God and the King of Salem. (See Hebrews 7:2)

Abram did not just defeat Kings, but he overthrew kingdoms. None of the kingdoms could stand the skill and the God of Abram in battle. The very same God is our God, and He is the same yesterday, today and forevermore. At the valley of Siddim, Yahweh and Abram prevailed against the kingdoms of the world. The systems of the world were beaten and overthrown and Abram brought about a revolution that the

Spiritual Revolution

world has never seen. It is time to arise and bring a revolution in our lives. It is time to overthrow satanic systems and replace them with the systems of our Heavenly Kingdom. Oh Lord, thy will be done on earth as it is in heaven.

The reason behind the war of the nine Kings

- Rebellion – after thirteen years of submission to Chedorlaomer, the five kings of the cities of the Jordan plain revolted against Chedorlaomer's rule (Elamite), their revolt started with refusing to pay tribute. In response, Chedorlaomer and three other rulers of Mesopotamia began a campaign against the Jordan plains.
- We see Abram defeating four kings that defeated the five kings, and he rescued his brother's son Lot and he brought back all the goods that Lot owned, as well as the women and the children.

"Then after Abram's return from the defeat (slaughter) of Chedorlaomer and the kings who were with him, the king of Sodom went out to meet him at the valley of Shaveh, (that is the King's Valley)" (Genesis 14:17 AMP).

After the victory then an encounter

After the defeat of Kings and victory over kingdoms, Abram encountered two kings.

Watch and Pray

Purpose of both encounters

1. Encounter with the King of Sodom

- The king of Sodom said to Abram, "Give back my people who were captured. But you may keep for yourself all the goods you have recovered." After deliverance of Lot and the people, the King of Sodom still came to demand the return of the people. Satan operates in the same way, he does not want you delivered, regardless of Jesus' death and resurrection to save and deliver the world. Abram as a type of Messiah, paid the price of warfare to save the captives, risking his life and that of his men. But the King of Sodom showed up and demanded the delivered people as if the price was not paid. Jesus paid the price sin required by leaving his throne in heaven, took the mortal body, lived and ate the food of humans, died for the remission of sin and resurrected to reconcile us back to God. He did everything necessary to save and reconcile everything and everyone back to God. But Satan still comes back as if no price was paid for our deliverance and salvation. The devil still makes people pay for what is theirs. In this verse, we see the spirit of Sodom in operation, the spirit of exploitation. Rise and pray against the spirit of exploitation against your life, whoever the Son of man has made free, is free indeed.

How to deal with the spirit of Sodom

Abram said to the king of Sodom, I have lifted up my hand unto the Lord, the Most High God, the possessor of the heavens and earth, that I will not take from you a thread, even

Spiritual Revolution

to a shoe-latchet; I will not take anything that is yours, lest you should say, I have made Abram rich. Abram rejected any collaboration with the King of Sodom, his no was a clear "No". Reject the enemy, let him know your position.

2. Abram's second encounter after Victory
- Abram had an encounter with the King of Salem and the Priest of Most High God, Melchizedek who brought forth bread and wine. He blessed him and said, Blessed be Abram of the Most High God, possessor of the heavens and earth, and blessed be the Most High God, who has delivered your enemies into your hand and Abram gave him tithes of all.
- The people we encounter in life come to give or collect from us. There are those who represent the Sodomic system or the Abrahamic system. It is time to drive out the Sodomic system and spirit out of our lives. Being exploited is not our portion in the name of Jesus Christ. Rebelliousness is not our portion in the name of Jesus Christ. Submission to devils and demons is not our portion in the name of Jesus Christ. Amen.
- There are people also in our lives who give to us, who bring us the Word of God, who bless us and pray for us, moreover, they bring bread and wine at the table to dine with us in the presence of the Lord our King. We must be guarded that the spirit of Sodom is not working through us to rebel and exploit those that the Lord has brought into our lives. We should be like a river, with an inflow and outflow. Then we will carry fresh water that will refresh whoever encounters us.

Watch and Pray

Significance of Melchizedek's Encounter

After victory over kings and kingdoms with an army of three hundred and eighteen trained servants, Melchizedek king of Salem met Abram.

Who is Melchizedek?

> And the promise became an Oath

- King of righteousness
- King of Salem - King of Peace
- Priest of the Most High God - Superior to Abram

The role of Melchizedek was to:

- Institute and announce the new order through Abram – He brought Abram to the Lord's table and introduced him to the Bread and Wine order.
- Bless he who had a promise – Melchizedek was superior to Abram, therefore, He was qualified to bless this great man, for the greater shall bless the lessor. He blessed him and said: Blessed be Abram of God Most High, Possessor of Heaven and Earth. And blessed be God Most High who has delivered your enemies into your hands. *And the promise became an Oath*, forever binding and still beneficial to whoever is connected to this great patriarch.

Spiritual Revolution

- Melchizedek collected the tithes of all the spoils to establish a pattern for the generations to come.
- Abram gave his tithes of all the spoils he received from battle, giving thanks to God who gave him victory and protection. This act between Melchizedek and Abram paints a picture of a God system. God wants us, the seed of Abram to adopt the Melchizedek order of giving our tithes and partake of the bread and the wine and use this act to replace the world system. The act of giving tithes and partaking of the communion meal separate us from all other belief systems. God revealed the kingdom system through Melchizedek and Abram a thousand of years before Jesus the bread from heaven is born and gave himself up for us. The system is revealed for the physical and spiritual seed of Abram to replenish, subdue and dominate the world and the market place.

Significance of bread

- The bread symbolizes the Word of God – the doctrine of the kingdom which Abram needed to be indoctrinated in order to establish God's Kingdom.
- Body of our Lord – reveals the body of our Lord Jesus Christ, which was slain before the foundation of the world, and will be manifested to the world in future.
- Instituted to distinguish those who belong to God through Christ.
- To declare a covenant with our God and the church
- To declare Jesus' Coming as a conquering King

Watch and Pray

- To remind the devil of his future – to expose the enemy of destiny and progress.

Significance of the Wine

- The wine symbolizes the spirit of the Kingdom. As God gives Abram principles that will govern His kingdom on the earth, He needs to give him His Spirit. Every throne has the spirit behind it, every position has the power backing it.
- The wine also symbolizes the blood of the new covenant through the shedding of the blood at the cross.

As Abram is endowed with the Word and the Spirit of the Kingdom, he will conquer all other kingdoms and systems of the world and replace satanic systems with the everlasting Godly system. *"This book of the law shall not depart from your mouth, but you shall meditate on it day and night, so that you may be careful to do according to all that is written in it. For then you will make your way prosperous, and then you will have good success" (Joshua 1:8 ESV).*

Why did the Sodomic King want to take the people and not the goods?

The Sodomic system exploits people while God's system restores, empowers and rewards people.

- Sodomic system knows that the greatest assets are people. Machines cannot be exploited; machines cannot invent or innovate. If you have people, you are wealthier than having assets and machines. Machines still need people to operate them.

Spiritual Revolution

- The Sodomic system takes from people instead of giving, it wants to receive and knows no honour.

Replacing the systems of the world

The systems of the world are in existence and are exploiting people including the church. We cannot freely give because we owe mortgage bonds, credit cards, and cars. We need to be empowered to cause a divine revolution in our lives, in our work place, and the market place.

You can never revolutionize your life unless you acquaint yourself with the system of your kingdom. Many of us claim to know the kingdom of our God and its power, while we are bound and restrained by the worldly system. It is time to break out! Lord, as you call us out of the world systems to God's Kingdom system, help us hear and know how to respond to the call. We need to be ambassadors of a kind of a system that rules and overthrows satanic systems and kingdoms of the world.

How to respond to the Sodomic System

"And Abram said to the king of Sodom, I have lift up mine hand unto the LORD, The Most High God, the possessor of heaven and earth, that I will not take from you a thread even to a shoe latchet, and that I will not take anything that is yours, lest you should say, I have made Abram rich" (Gen 14:22-23 KJV).

Abram refused to cooperate and partner in anyway with the King of Sodom: I will not take from you anything lest you should say, my system has made Abram rich: moreover, I have sacrificed myself and the lives of these men to set free the

Watch and Pray

captives, therefore, I will not be the one to hand the people over to bondage again. I have sworn unto the Lord that I am a believer, and He can trust me with nations. I will not compromise my relationship with God for you, king of Sodom.

We see God sustaining Abram throughout his life. Regardless of the challenges that pursued him and his family. He grew from strength to strength. Moreover, he grew in the knowledge of God and His name became great. Today, the nations of the world are fighting to be called the seed of Abraham.

> *"Integrity and honesty will protect me because I wait for you" (Psalm 25:21)*

CHAPTER EIGHT

DO NOT FORGET WHAT THE ENEMY DID TO YOU...
Exodus 17:8

The battle began in the womb

"[Two] children struggled together within her; and she said, if it so [that the Lord has heard our prayer], why am I like this? And she went to inquire of the Lord" (Genesis 25:22 AMPC).

The Lord said to her, two nations are in your womb, and the separation of two people has begun in your body; the one people shall be stronger than the other, and the elder shall serve the younger. When her days to be delivered were fulfilled, behold there were twins in her womb. The first one came out red all over like a hairy garment, and they named him Esau. Afterward his brother came forth, and his hand grasped Esau's heel; so he was named Jacob.

The battle of the two nations was revealed while Rebekah was still pregnant with the twins, Esau and Jacob. The battle outlived them and streamed to their descendants.

Watch and Pray

Who is Amalek?

"And Timna was a concubine of Eliphaz, Esau's son and she bore Amalek to Eliphaz....Amalek was the son of Eliphaz and her mother was Eliphaz's concubine named Timna, the grandson of Esau the son of Isaac" (Genesis 36:12, 16; 1 Chronicles 1:35-36 AMP).

What did the Amalek do to Israel?

During the Exodus of the Israelites from Egypt, Amalek attacked Israel while they were on route to the Promised Land. Amalek was the first enemy that Israel encountered after crossing the Red sea. When the nations of the world heard about the miracles the Lord has done for the deliverance of Israel from slavery, the nations feared the Lord and His people. No nation dared to attack them, but Amalek did not fear the Lord.

The Amalek challenged God

"I will harden (make stubborn, strong) Pharaoh's heart, that he will pursue them, and I will gain honor and glory over Pharaoh and all his host, and the Egyptians shall know that I AM the Lord" (Exodus 14:4 AMPC).

The deliverance of Israel from Egypt to the Promise Land was God's battle and not Israel's. God said to Moses, I have surely heard the cry of my people in Egypt because of their task masters, and I have come to deliver them. God himself came to deliver Israel, though human eyes saw Moses and Aaron.

The promise of God to Abraham was about to be fulfilled, and Amalek decided to challenge the throne of God by attacking Israel on their way to the promise land.

Do not Forget what the Enemy Did to you

The Amalekites Attack Israel

The Amalekites came and attacked the Israelites at Rephidim. Moses said to Joshua, "Choose some of our men and go out to fight the Amalekites. Tomorrow I will stand on top of the hill with the staff of God in my hands." So Joshua fought the Amalekites as Moses had ordered, and Moses, Aaron and Hur went to the top of the hill. As long as Moses held up his hands, the Israelites were winning, but whenever he lowered his hands, the Amalekites were winning. When Moses' hands grew tired, they took a stone and put it under him and he sat on it. Aaron and Hur held his hands up – one on one side, one on the other – so that his hands remained steady till sunset. So Joshua overcame the Amalekite army with the sword. Then the Lord said to Moses, "Write this on a scroll as something to be remembered and make sure that Joshua hears it, because I will completely blot out the name of Amalek from under heaven." Moses built an altar and called it "The Lord is my Banner". He said, "Because hands were lifted up against the throne of the Lord, the Lord will be at war against the Amalekites from generation to generation" (Exodus 17:16)." Rephidim means Support or Rest – Amalek attacked Israel at the place of rest, where Israel had no water to drink. People were thirsty and needed support; they needed water to refresh themselves.

"Behold I will stand before you there on the rock at Mount Horeb; and you shall strike the rock, and water shall come out of it, that the people may drink. And Moses did so in the sight of the elders of Israel" (Exodus 17:6 NKJV).

Watch and Pray

When the water started to flow, Amalek attacked the weary, the thirsty and those who were behind.

The sin of the Amalek

- He feared not the Lord
- They lifted their hand against the throne of God
- They attacked Israel at the place of Rest
- Attacked the feeble and the thirsty when God has actually provided the water to be refreshed (enjoy the miracle of provision)

DO NOT FORGET - Deuteronomy 25:17-19

"Remember what Amalek did unto thee by the way, when ye were come forth out of Egypt; how he met thee by the way, and smote the hindmost of thee, even all that were feeble behind thee, when thou was faint and weary; and he feared not God. Therefore, it shall be, when the LORD thy God hath given thee rest from all thine enemies round about, in the land which the LORD thy God giveth thee for an inheritance to possess it, that thou shalt blot out the remembrance of Amalek from under heaven; thou shalt not forget it."

A clear mandate for Moses, Joshua and all Israel

Keep the records

Do not forget what Amalek did to you. This lesson is for the church today. We should not forget what Satan did to us, our families and nations. Moreover, what he did at Calvary, Satan meant to shame the church, but little did he know that it was a setup. He didn't know that the death of Jesus at Calvary was changing the order for the living and the dead. His plan

Do not Forget what the Enemy Did to you

was to shame while God's plan was to save. The enemy will attack and shame you when you are weak and need mercy, but God covers and protects in moment of weakness.

Restoration agenda in progress

Once you forget what the enemy did to you, you are likely to be trapped and wiped out by the same. If you forget what you have lost, you are likely to miss the pay-back time, which is your restoration. Moreover, you are likely to fall into the same trap again and again. Judges 2:10 reminds us that Joshua and his generation died and a new generation rose after them, which knew not the Lord, nor yet the works which he had done for Israel. And the new generation of the children of Israel did evil in the sight of the Lord, and served Baalim. And God delivered them into the hands of their spoilers. Instead of enjoying the Promise Land, the children of Israel were distressed because they forgot the Lord their God, and his wonderful works.

They forgot why they were in the Promise Land; they forgot the pain their fathers went through in Egypt; they forgot that some people lost their children in Egypt; they forgot that Moses sacrificed his life and never stepped into the Promise Land because of them. Do not forget that some people sacrificed their lives, education, families and pleasures for the freedom of our countries. Other people sacrificed their lives for the gospel, *do not forget…*

Watch and Pray

The mandate is clear

Go attack the Amalek, (operation WIPE OUT)

Jehovah God has been a faithful God and King to Israel since the time of Abraham. He revealed the migration to and from Egypt to Abraham four hundred years earlier. When Israel settled in the Promise Land, they demanded for a human king like the nations of the world. God approved the ordination of King Saul, to take over from Him. The new king that was taking over Israel from King Jehovah, was to carry out and settle pending battles of God such as wiping out the memory of the Amalekites from under heaven.

King Saul was not yet born and was not at Rephidim at the time of the Exodus and never experienced any attack by Amalek. But this battle was beyond Saul, it is a generational battle, it is God's battle. Saul as a new King must be careful to carry the mandate with passion like he was there when Amalek lifted his hand against the throne of God. He must hold Amalek accountable and must ensure that he is brought to task for his behaviour during the days of the Exodus. Moses is gone, Joshua is gone, but the Ancient of Days is still around. He remembers what the enemy did to his weary, thirsty and feeble people.

"Samuel also said to Saul, "The Lord sent me to anoint you king over His people, Israel. Now therefore, heed the voice of the words of the Lord. 2 Thus says the Lord of hosts: 'I will punish Amalek for what he did to Israel, how he ambushed him on the way when he came up from Egypt. 3 Now go and attack Amalek, and utterly destroy all that they have, and

Do not Forget what the Enemy Did to you

do not spare them. But kill both man and woman, infant and nursing child, ox and sheep, camel and donkey" (1 Samuel 15:1-3 NKJV).

"And Saul attacked the Amalekites, from Havilah all the way to Shur, which is east of Egypt. He also took Agag king of the Amalekites alive, and utterly destroyed all the people with the edge of the sword. But Saul and the people spared Agag and the best of the sheep, the oxen, the fatlings, the lambs, and all that was good, and were unwilling to utterly destroy them. But everything despised and worthless, that they utterly destroyed" (1 Samuel 15:7-9 NKJV).

Saul indeed went and attacked Amalek. He partially implemented the plan. Partial obedience is disobedience, and such acts caught up with the Israelites later. When it's time to wipe out your enemy, do so unapologetically. When God has given you an advantage over your enemy, use it. If you do not wipe him out, he will wipe you out. And right now God has commanded His angels to carry out the mandate of wiping out every enemy of your peace and establishment. The Lord remembers what the devil did to you when you were weak, when you needed mercy, when you needed the opportunity, when you needed financial breakthrough. The devil stole your car, your marriage, you are in debts, you lost your assets and now it is time to Wipe-Out the enemy.

Sometimes we give mercy where it is not due, that is why when the enemy gets an opportunity to destroy the righteous, he attacks with a series of outbreaks that intends to finish you off. We should learn to do the same as a church.

Watch and Pray

CHAPTER NINE

VALLEY EXPERIENCES

A VALLEY is defined as a low area between hills or mountains. In this chapter, I would like to define the valley as the low seasons in a person's or believer's life. In the valley, a person experiences a series of unpleasant situations and afflictions. Valleys are a battle field whereby children of God are confronted by the opposition with limited answers or solutions. Life can lead us to different valleys and the valley experience demands a response from each and every one of us. The hand of the Lord was upon Ezekiel and carried him out in the spirit of the Lord and set him in the midst of the valley which was full of bones, and caused him to pass by them round about: and behold, there were very many in the open valley: and, lo, they were very dry.

Ezekiel did not take himself to the valley, it was not by choice that he found himself in the valley. The valley he found himself in had bones, these bones were many. Not only that, they were dry, meaning, they were lifeless. Ezekiel had lifeless bones in front of him, he had to respond to the question that the situation was asking of him, Son of man, can these bones live? You and I today are confronted by conditions and

Watch and Pray

situations that are asking the same questions to us, can this situation change? Can we be healed? Can I ever find peace? Will my marriage survive this? Will my child come out of drugs alive? Can this virus be defeated without losing our people? Ezekiel, like you and me, were required to respond, O Lord God, thou knowest. There are times in life where we will be confronted by situations beyond our knowledge and understanding. Ezekiel acknowledged that only God knows, he surrendered his limited knowledge and ability and allowed God's knowledge to take precedence. As he was in the hopeless valley, with a lifeless situation. God gave him an instruction to prophesy to the situation. He didn't prophesy on behalf of God without God, he acted on His instruction.

As he prophesied, there was a noise, and behold a shaking, and the bones came together, bone to this bone. As the prophet beheld, lo, the sinews and the flesh came up upon them, and skin covered them above: but there was no breath in them. Then the Lord instructed Ezekiel to prophesy unto the wind, and say to the wind, thus saith the Lord God; come from the four winds, O breath, and breathe upon these slain, that they may live. So I prophesied as he commanded me, and the breath came into them, and they lived, and stood up upon their feet, an exceeding great army. Hallelujah! A valley experience and season is not the place of doom and gloom. But a platform to show forth the power of the Kingdom. The dry bones in the valley looked hopeless yet they were an exceeding great army that had been silenced. The prophet didn't know that God has put the resurrection power of the exceeding great army in his tongue. The life and the faith of the prophet was changed at the valley. Jesus is the rose of Sharon, the Lily of

Valley Experiences

the valley. When we experience different valleys in our lives, remember that Jesus Christ's instructions and obedience is very central to experiencing your turnaround. The Omnipresent God is with you to guide you in your valley. (See Songs of songs 2:1).

The God of the Mountains is Still God in the Valleys.

There are different types of valleys in the Bible, which signify different situations in our lives. In this chapter, we are going to look at the following Valleys.

Valley of the Shadow of Death

It is said that, the old Roman Road to Jericho, which was used by our Lord Jesus (Mark 10:32), leaves the modern road from Jerusalem just beyond the Hotel of the Good Samaritan. It emerges close to the location of the Roman who lived in Jericho in Jesus' time. The road is narrow and twisted following a water path, with cliffs rising on both sides. David as a shepherd used this valley as he travelled with his flock. It is still used today by shepherds. Everyday David had to trust God for protection hence he said even though I walk through the valley of the shadow of the death, I will fear no evil. David was passing through the physical valley, where death was possible because of the falling rocks and wild animals etc. Today the valley of the shadow of death might be spiritual, sickness, poverty or other situations that we face as people.

In the valley of the shadow of death, where your life is threatened by danger and death, the rod and the staff of the Lord is there to protect you. Arise and declare, the Lord is my shepherd. (See Psalm 23).

Watch and Pray

The Valley of Siddim

This valley is on the spot where the cities of Sodom and Gomorrah were. This is the valley where sin thrived. It represents the valley of sin in our lives.

Then Jehovah rained upon Sodom and upon Gomorrah brimstone and fire from Jehovah out of heaven to judge the prevalent sin. (See Genesis 19:24).

When we find ourselves trapped in sin, God is there to deliver us by the blood of His Son Jesus, that was shed for the remission of our sins. If you find yourself trapped in this valley do not condemn yourself and give in to eternal judgement. God loves you enough to forgive all your sins. Confess them to him in prayer, repent and don't look back. Everyone who shall call on the name of Jesus shall be saved. Confess the book of Psalm 51 and you shall feel the weight of sin being lifted from your life.

The Valley of Jezreel

It is the largest valley in Israel and divides the Mountains of Galilee in the north and those of Samaria in the south. This valley has a history of many wars as invading armies of the Pharaohs of Egypt, Hittites, Philistines, Assyrians, Syrians, Persians, Greeks, Romans, Crusaders, Turks and British have marched and fought on its broad plain.

This valley is important in scripture, because in the valley of Jezreel the end-time battle shall be fought. Russia will come on the valley of Jezreel and fight against Palestine. Egypt will come from the South to the same valley and fight against Palestine. China will come from the east to the valley of Jezreel

Valley Experiences

and fight against Palestine. In this valley, the armies of the world will be gathered together in the great end time battle. Russia and her horses, a Great Calvary, and the nations of the east and north shall be gathered together in this valley against Palestine. The western powers, the US, England and the Roman Empire will come and fight against Russia in the valley of Jezreel.

It will be the scene of the battle, Armageddon (See Revelation 16:13-16). Judges 6:33 and 7:1-22 describes the victory of Gideon and his three hundred men over the host of the Midianites in this valley with their trumpets, lamps and they cry, *"The sword of the Lord and of Gideon"*. We can learn the lesson that when we're on God's side, we're on the winning side.

Mass attacks may come against you, but our God has all figured out. He is on the throne, and in full control.

The Valley of Kidron/Valley of Jehoshaphat

The Valley of Kidron is nearly 3 kilometres long. It is situated east of the wall of Jerusalem, between the ancient city and the Mount of Olives. This is the Valley of suffering. And is also a valley where many great giants of Israel were buried like Samson, James, and possibly Samuel.

It is also the Valley and the place where Jesus will assemble the nations for judgment as He introduces His Glorious Kingdom reign.

"I will gather all nations, and will bring them down into the valley of Jehoshaphat; and I will execute judgment upon them there for my people and for my heritage Israel, whom they have scattered among the nations: and they have parted my land" (Joel 3:12 ASV).

Watch and Pray

We should remember that it was this same valley that the Lord crossed as He went out to Gethsemane and agonised before His Father in view of the sufferings of the cross.

Summon all your spiritual enemies to this valley and execute Judgement in Jesus name, for everything you suffered and went through. This is the place for judgement and the time is now.

The Valley of Eschol

This Valley is located just inside the promise land; the valley produced great clusters of grapes, so much that they called the brook nearby, "Eschol" meaning "clusters of grapes". A branch with one cluster had to be carried between two men "upon a staff".

"And they came unto the valley of Eshcol, and cut down from thence a branch with one cluster of grapes, and they bare it upon a staff between two; they brought also of the pomegranates, and of the figs. That place was called the valley of Eshcol, because of the cluster which the children of Israel cut down from thence" Numbers 13:23-24 ASV).

It was at this Valley where Israel had to make a decision to either move forward or not, especially after the report of discouragement from the ten spies. In our daily lives we are confronted by the valley of decision making. As you are caught up between your Canaan and the Giants in your Canaan, know that the Lord is "able to do exceedingly abundantly above all that we can ask or think". He is a bountiful God. Do not allow the Giants in the land to stop you, for your God is a Gigantic God.

Valley Experiences

The Valley of Elah

This is the valley of battles, where the Giant Goliath and his taunting and mockery of the Israelites was going on for forty days. In this valley, David came with his sling and stone to slay him. Throughout the battles of life, know that the Lord is right there to direct your sling and stone to slay the Giants attacking your life. Fear not, the taunting of the Giants is meant to make you panic and lose focus; your God is the only God who knows yesterday, today and the future.

Goliath mocked Israel for forty days and forty nights, in scripture, the number forty symbolizes a number of probation. This was the confirmation that Goliath's battle against God's people had expired. Battles in God's schedule are not supposed to go beyond forty days. It is important to pay attention to the importance of numbers, because they carry a spiritual meaning that could be a key to unlock doors of your life and destiny.

The Valley of Rephaim

This is the valley of the Giants, and David repeatedly had to confront and fight his Philistine enemies there (See 2 Sam. 5:18,19, 22; 1 Chron. 14:9).

To David, the Valley of Giants, became a place of Breakthrough, he named this place Baalperazim. For us to experience continuous victory, we should not stop enquiring of the Lord in our valleys.

"The Philistines also came and spread themselves in the valley of Rephaim. And David enquired of the LORD, saying, Shall I go up to the Philistines? wilt thou deliver them into mine hand? And the LORD said unto David, Go up: for I will doubtless deliver the Philistines into

Watch and Pray

thine hand. And David came to Baalperazim, and David smote them there, and said, The LORD hath broken forth upon mine enemies before me, as the breach of waters. Therefore he called the name of that place Baalperazim" (2 Samuel 5:18 -20 ASV).

The Valley of Ajalon

The name means "a chain" or "strength". Here Joshua called on the Lord to assist him in his battle with the Amorites who inhabited the valley. Trusting God, Joshua said in the sight of Israel, *"Sun, stand thou still upon Gibeon; and thou, Moon, in the Valley of Ajalon, and the sun stood still and the moon stayed, until the people had avenged themselves upon their enemies."* Joshua 10:14 tells us that *"there was no day like that before it or after it, that the Lord hearkened unto the voice of a man". (See Joshua 10:12 KJV).*

In the midst of the battle, time was not favouring Joshua and his army; Joshua remembered that there is a Lily in his valley. Arise and command time to favour you, until you get the victory you deserve.

Valley of Baca

This is the Valley of Weeping, there are tears in many eyes, enough to make a well, pain and twinges in the hearts of men, but today the Lord is saying, you are passing through this valley. For you are anointed to go through the valley. And you are moving from strength to strength, you are growing stronger by day. Remember, weeping may endure for the night, but joy comes in the morning.

"Blessed is the man whose strength is in thee; in whose heart are the highways to Zion. Passing through the valley of Weeping they make it a place of springs; yea, the early rain covereth it with blessings. They go from

Valley Experiences

strength to strength; every one of them appeareth before God in Zion" (Psalm 84:5-7 KJV).

Valley of Salt

"And David [belved] got [him] a name when he returned from attacking of the Aram [Syrians] in the Valley of Salt, [being] eighteen thousand [men]" (2 Samuel 8:13 NMV).

This is the valley of permanent burial of the enemy. When the enemy is buried in salt he can never rise again.

Declare and say, *"I summon every enemy of progress in my life to the valley of salt for battle".*

- I hide my life in the blood of Jesus, as I engage in this battle.
- I attack and destroy all enemies of progress (name them) in Jesus name.
- I bury all my enemies in salt, and I declare that they will never rise again, in Jesus name. Amen!

The Valley of Achor

This refers to one of the valleys running into the hills behind Jericho. It was a very fruitful place of corn and cattle. This is the valley where Israel lost its battle against Ai, as a result of Achan's sin. It is a valley of punishment and chastening where Achan and his family were stoned to death.

The name of this Valley means "a door of hope" and from here the children of Israel were able to press on with hope and encouragement into the Promise Land. How good it is to press on pleasing the Lord, after defeat caused by others.

Watch and Pray

"And I will give her, her vineyards from thence, and the valley of Achor for a door of hope; and she shall make answer there, as in the days of her youth, and as in the day when she came up out of the land of Egypt" (Hosea 2:15 ASV).

Valley of Hinnom/Gehenna

This valley on the south side of Jerusalem has a very dreadful history. It is the place where idolatrous Jews burned their children alive to Moloch, Baal and the Sun. It is also called the Valley of Tophet from "Toph", meaning an instrument of loud sound which was beaten like a drum to drown the cries of the victims. King Josiah made the valley a container for the rubbish of the city. In it a fire was kept continually burning and it became an emblem of hell (See Matthew 5:22; Isaiah 30:33).

"For a Topheth is prepared of old; yea, for the king it is made ready; he hath made it deep and large; the pile thereof is fire and much wood; the breath of Jehovah, like a stream of brimstone, doth kindle it" (Isaiah 30:33 ASV).

God will certainly judge idolatry for His name is Jealous. Make a decision to worship the living God. Salvation is not salvation if it is not confessed with one's mouth and believed in the heart. Let us escape this valley and be vigilant at all times. Praying for the nations of the world to come to the knowledge of God.

Valley and battlefields

Valley experiences are not easy, but necessary for growth, testimonies and encounters with God. There is no mountain without valleys. Pick yourself up from your valley (battlefield),

Valley Experiences

because the mountain life (promotion and victory) is in front of you. In every valley that you might be facing today, you are anointed to go through it. Valley experiences do not last forever but are there for a season, to usher in your breakthroughs. Amen.

Watch and Pray

CHAPTER TEN

GOD'S KAIROS REVEALED

Kairos is an ancient Greek word meaning the right moment when something must be done.

Everything has its own time and season, everything has to wait for its turn to manifest,

The account of Genesis 1 reveals a profound lesson and is a testimony of Ecclesiastes 3.

Time is a subject in God's creation.

God has given his children authority over time, to reverse unwanted events, correct the errors of the past, recreate and bring future events to the present.

It is evident from scripture that creation itself was measured by time. From the first day of creation to the seventh day when God rested, time was used as a quantifying instrument. If God could set timelines for his own work, this should teach us to set time-lines for our goals. This same system is used today in the corporate world. Institutions of learning use time tables; hospitals also uses time tables, even the church needs to have a manifestation and implementation plan (set times) for the activities of the ministry. This could be the perfect way to understand God's Kairos.

Example of God's Manifestation Plan (Kairos)

God has set times for everything that need to happen on earth. The first set time I would like to refer to is the:

- **Dispensation of Angels**: there was a time where God created angels. He had a Kairos plan when angels were created, heaven and earth were created. He also had Kiaros plan when angels would betray the kingdom. It was already in the schedule of manifestation. God knew before he created angels that one day Lucifer will betray the Kingdom and He already had a salvation plan in place to save us all (See Isaiah 14:12).

God re-created the earth, and He rested from creation work on the seventh day.

- **Dispensation of Innocence**: From recreation to the fall (See Genesis 2:15-3:31).
- Dispensation of Conscience: from the fall to the flood (See Genesis 3:22-8:14).
- **Dispensation of Human Government**: from the flood to the call of Abraham (Genesis 8:15 -11:32).
- **Dispensation of Promise**: From the call of Abraham to the Exodus from Egypt (See Genesis 12:1 -Exodus 12:37).
- **Dispensation of the Law**: from the Exodus to the preaching of John the Baptist (See Exodus 12:38- Matthew 2:23).

God's Kairos Revealed

- **Dispensation of Grace**: From the Preaching of John to the second Coming of Christ (See Mathew 3:1 - Revelation 19:10).
- **Rapture of the Church**: at least seven years before the end of the age of grace (See Matthew 3:1-Revelation 19:10).
- **The Tribulation Period**: Beginning of Daniel's 70th week of the 2nd coming (See Daniel 9:27, Revelation 19:11-21).
- **Dispensation of Divine Government**: from the 2nd Coming to the New Heavens and New Earth (See Revelation 19:11 - 20:15).
- **Dispensation of Faithful Angels and the Redeemed**: Throughout all Eternity (See Revelation 21-22).

From God's set times above, we are able to see where we are, and where we are going. These set times that appear in God's Manifestation plan must come to pass because they are appointed times. God honours *SET TIMES*. When do you want your miracles to take place? Do you have a plan for all your desires? If you can die today, can your successors run with what you have started? Our Ministries, inventions and good works, should outlive us. When you are gone, your works should speak of you and your faith. Elisha, Joshua, Mary and Moses are no more, but their works are alive through every generation.

Watch and Pray

The Solar system created

"And God said, let there be lights in the firmament of the heaven to divide the day from the night; and let them be for signs, and for seasons, and for days, and years: And let them be for lights in the firmament of the heaven to give light upon the earth: and it was so. And God made two great lights; the greater light to rule the day, and the lesser light to rule the night: he made the stars also. And God set them in the firmament of the heaven to give light upon the earth, and to rule over the day and over the night, and to divide the light from the darkness: and God saw that it was good. And the evening and the morning were the fourth day" (Gen 1:14-19 ASV).

We learn from the Word that; God spoke time into existence. He also created the Terminator, which is the line that separates night from the day.

The purpose of time is to mark seasons, days and years. Time measures life span of anything. Without time you can never know the lifespan of a thing or a person. Anything that is not time bound is eternal. God gave man the authority over times and seasons, to reverse and to forward spiritual activities that affect human life. Everything that is time bound has an expiry date. Meaning, it will never last forever. Be rest assured that God is the author of time and He lives outside time. Only beings that live outside time can influence and control time. As a matter of fact, time lives in him.

The devil is a spirit being that has been detached from the realm of authority over time, to a realm of authority of time. He is in a territory of time. He was demoted from heaven hence he is bound by time.

God's Kairos Revealed

"Therefore rejoice, ye heavens, and ye that dwell in them. Woe to the inhibiters of the earth and of the sea! for the devil is come down unto you, having great wrath, because he knoweth that he hath but a short time" (Revelation 12:12 ASV).

The church and believers are lifted by Christ's death and resurrection, time has got no hold over us, unless we allow it.

"And hath raised us up together, and made us sit together in heavenly places in Christ Jesus" (Ephesians 2:6 ASV).

Kairos revealed

God has appointed time for everything. If God did not appoint times, the bible would have not mentioned which day God created what He created. It would simply mention that God created. For that reason, that the Word of God mentions the creation story indicating days when everything was made, it shows the significance thereof. It is stated in the Word of God that on the seventh day God rested. This is God's set time to rest. You can agree to the fact that God truly has appointed and set times and seasons for everything as recorded in Genesis 1.

Jesus could have died for mankind as soon as Adam and Eve sinned. But because of God's set time, Jesus had to wait for the fullness of time to manifest. This does not mean that God was still going to think of a plan to redeem the world, but He already had the Plan. The ability to wait is a skill that defeats and frustrates the enemy.

You know, the devil's followers concluded that God has been defeated by Satan, no wonder the judgement of the devil is still pending. They think that God is still planning how to

Watch and Pray

implement the hell story. Little do they know that it is a matter of Kairos, rather than planning and strategizing. That is why Satan's followers worship him. They believe satan is the hero. When the fullness of time comes, satan and his followers will be wiped away forever in a *"Lake of Fire"*. His verdict can never change even if he repents. And satan knows it, no wonder he is using deception as a weapon to deceive many.

At the cross, Jesus looked defeated in the eyes of the enemy. He was quiet when the enemy mocked and accused him; the Master knew that he could not defeat the enemy by debating and defending himself. You might look defeated but that does not mean you are! Jesus was arrested, mocked, and beaten not because He could not finish the Roman Soldiers at once with one blow of His breath, but because it was necessary to remain humble and fulfil the salvation plan. To me, humility is knowing but still learning from others who know less than you; humility is being able to wait for your turn even when you are not supposed to wait. Knowing very well that you have the power, the resources, the contacts, but you decide to wait and be quiet about it, until your turn presents itself to act; that ability to wait, calmly is humility displayed. You may have to wait for your blessings to manifest, remember waiting does not mean denial.

Let us confess together and say: *"Oh God, grant me the heart to wait and be patient, while you are at work in my life"*, in Jesus name. I might look defeated throughout the process of waiting; help me Lord to remember that, it is impossible to be defeated in Jesus Christ's name. Amen.

God's Kairos Revealed

Ecclesiastes 3:1 testifies that there is time for everything.

"For the vision is yet for an appointed time, but at the end it shall speak, and not lie: though it tarry, wait for it; because it will surely come, it will not tarry" (Habakkuk 2:3 KJV).

The appointed times of the lord

Before the actual event, God gives his people a foretaste (preview). Before the Israelites could occupy the promise land, they tasted the fruits of the land first. Before Jesus could come and die for the sins of the world, God used men as a type of Christ to reveal his plan. We see this through the situations patriarchs and matriarchs faced and the victories they received. One needs a basic understanding of how God uses the principle of a Shadow to reveal the Substance. The feasts of the Lord/Jews fulfilled in Christ become the promises God makes to the Church.

Let us view the 7 feasts of the Lord and their relevance to the Church today.

The Feasts of the Lord

The Word FEAST means "SET TIME" (kairos times)

Leviticus 23 gives an account of the *"Seven Great Feasts"* of the Lord. They were a prophecy and foreshadowing of future events, part of which have been fulfilled, and other parts are yet to be. They are *the "shadow of things to come"* of which Christ is the substance. (See Colossians 2:16-17). They were instituted by the Lord. The people had no opinion in the matter. God promised that if the males went up at the "set time" to Jerusalem to keep these Feasts, He would look after their families. When the people became formal and indifferent, the Lord said, *"Your new moons and your appointed Feasts, My soul Hateth; they are a Trouble unto Me; I am weary to bear them"* (Isaiah 1:14 ASV). Therefore, Jesus called them the *"Feasts of the Jews,"* rather than the *"Feasts of the Lord."*

The *"Feasts of the Lord"* are seven in number. If we include the Sabbath they are eight. But the Sabbath stands by itself. It was to be observed weekly, the other Feasts annually. The Sabbath was to be observed at home, while the other Feasts were to be observed in Jerusalem. The *"Seven Feasts"* may be divided into two sections of four and three. The first section includes the **Passover, the Feasts of Unleavened Bread, Feast of First-Fruits and the Pentecost**. Then there was an interval of four months, followed by the **Feasts of the Trumpets, Day of Atonement, and Tabernacles**. The Three Great Festivals were the Passover, Pentecost, and Tabernacles. They extended from the 14th day of the First Month to the 22nd day of the Seventh Month.

The First Four Feasts foreshadow truths connected with this present Gospel Dispensation and those who form the heavenly people of the Lord, and the Church; while the last three Feasts foreshadow the blessings in store for God's earthly people, the Jews.

1. The Passover Feast

The LORD'S Passover: On the fourteenth day of the first month at twilight is the LORD'S Passover. *(This marks the day Jesus was to be crucified, fulfilled in 31 Ad).*

God's Kairos Revealed

Applying the Blood

The Passover Feast had its origin in Egypt. It was the memorial of the redemption and deliverance of the Children of Israel from Egypt. It was to them the beginning of months, and their birthday as a Nation. (See Exodus 12:2). It consisted of the taking of a male lamb, without blemish, of the first year, a lamb for a family and killing it on the 14th day of the month in the evening, and sprinkling its blood, with a bunch of hyssop, on the two side posts and upper lintel of the door of their houses, so that when the Lord passed through Egypt that night and saw the blood on the doorposts, He would spare the first born sheltered within. The flesh of the lamb was to be roasted and eaten with unleavened bread and bitter herbs, and none of it left until the morning. Those who ate of it were to do so with their loins girded, their shoes on their feet, and their staff in their hand, ready to leave Egypt.

Watch and Pray

The Passover Feast was to be to them as a Memorial, and they were to keep it as a Feast throughout their generations, and as an ordinance forever. (See Exodus 12:14).

The Passover Lamb was intended as a type of Jesus, the Lamb of God.

The shedding of His blood at Calvary, and our applying it in our lives by faith, has the same effect as to our Salvation, as the applying of the Passover Lamb's blood to the doorposts of those Israelites houses, they had to for the safety of those who were sheltered within. As that night was the beginning of months to them; so, the moment a soul accepts Jesus Christ as its Saviour, that moment it is born again, and a new life begins; for Christ, our Passover was sacrificed for us. (See 1 Corinthians 5:7).

The first time the Children of Israel observed the Passover Feast it was amidst the terrors of God's judgment plagues in the land of Egypt, a type of the world. Thereafter, its yearly observance was as a joyful Memorial of their deliverance from Egypt. The Christian Church does not observe the Passover, but they do observe it as a Memorial the ordinance of the Lord's Supper that Christ instituted in its place.

- Death, viruses, diseases, poverty, failure, frustration, divorce, sickness and any form assassination they are all skipping your home by the power of the blood of Jesus applied over your life and home. Amen.

God's Kairos Revealed

2. The Feast of Unleavened Bread

The Feast of Unleavened Bread began on the day after the Passover, and continued for seven days (See Leviticus 23:6-8). The lamb was slain on the 14th day at twilight, which ended the day. The Feast of Unleavened Bread began immediately after sunset, which was the beginning of the 15th day. Thus there was no interval between them. As the Passover is a type of the death of Christ, so the Feast of the Unleavened Bread is a type of the walk of the Believer, and there should be no interval between the salvation of a soul and its entrance on a holy life and walk. The seven days, point to the complete path of the Believer's life after conversion.

Leaven in the Scriptures is a type of evil or sin, so the Feast was to be kept with unleavened bread. (See Exodus 13:7). Paul speaks of malice and wickedness as leaven. Purge out therefore, the old leaven that ye may be a new lump, as ye are unleavened. For even Christ our Passover is sacrificed for us. *"Therefore, let us keep the Feast, not with old leaven, neither with the leaven of malice and wickedness, but with the unleavened bread of sincerity and truth"* (1 Corinthians 5:7-8 KJV).

The-typical teaching, then of the Feast of Unleavened Bread is that, having been saved by the shed blood of Christ, our Passover, we are to walk in newness of life. Purging out the leaven of worldliness, and doing no work that is done to earn salvation. We are saved by grace and not works!

3. The Feast of First-Fruits.

The Passover - took place on the 14th day of the month, the Feast of Unleavened Bread on the next day, which was the

Watch and Pray

Sabbath, and the following day, which was the morrow after the Sabbath, the Feast of First Fruits was to be celebrated. This Feast however, could not be done until after the Children of Israel had entered Canaan, therefore the Feast of First Fruits was not observed during the Wilderness Wanderings. The Offering was a sheaf reaped from the waving fields of the ripened harvest, and carried to the priest to be waved before the Lord for acceptance, and was to be followed by a Burnt, Meat and Drink Offering, but no Sin-Offering. The Burnt-Offering was to be a male lamb without blemish of the first year.

The Feast of First-Fruits was a type and foreshadowing of the Resurrection of Christ.

He arose on the morning after the Sabbath, and His resurrection is spoken of by Paul, as the First-Fruits of the resurrection of the dead. As the Corn of Wheat (See John 12:24) He was buried in Joseph's Tomb, and His resurrection was the First-Fruits of the Harvest of those who will be Christ's at His coming. (See 1 Corinthians 15:23).

When the Priest on the day of Christ's resurrection waved the sheaf of First-Fruits in the Temple, it was before a rent veil, and was, but an empty form, for the substance had come and the shadow had passed away, and the empty tomb of Joseph proclaimed that the Great First-Fruits' Sheaf had been reaped and waved in the Heavenly Temple. There will be no Feast of First Fruits in the Millennium, it has been fulfilled in Christ.

God's Kairos Revealed

4. The Feast of Pentecost.

Fifty days after the Feast of First-Fruits, the Feast of Pentecost was observed. The space between the two Feasts, which included Seven Sabbaths, was called the "Feast of Weeks." It began with the offering of the First-Fruits of the Barley Harvest, and ended with the ingathering of the Wheat Harvest. The First Day was the Feast of the First-Fruits, the Last Day was the Feast of Pentecost. Only the First and Last day were celebrated.

At the Feast of Pentecost, a New Meat Offering was to be offered before the Lord. It was called "new" because it must be of grain from the "new" harvest. At the Feast of First-Fruits stalks of grain were to be offered and waved, but at the Feast of Pentecost the grain was to be ground and made into flour, from which two loaves were to be baked with leaven. *The two loaves represent the two classes of people that were to form the Church, the Jews and Gentiles, and as believers are not perfect, even though saved, that imperfection is represented by the leaven.*

A "Burnt Offering" of seven lambs without blemish of the first year, one young bullock, and two rams, were to be offered with the "Wave Loaves", as well as "Meat" and "Drink" Offerings for a sweet savour unto the Lord. These were to be followed by a "Sin Offering" of a kid of the goats, and two lambs of the first year for a "Peace Offering." The "Wave Loaves" were to be waved before the Lord. Note that it is now "loaves" not loose stalks of grain. The "loaves" represent the homogeneousness of the Church.

Watch and Pray

The Feast of Pentecost had its fulfilment on the Day of Pentecost, when the disciples of the Lord were baptized into one body by the Holy Spirit (See 1 Corinthians 12:13).

The Interval

Between the Feast of Pentecost and the Feast of Trumpets, there was an interval of four months during which the Harvest and Vintage were gathered in. There was no convocation of the people during those busy months. This long "Interval" typifies the "Present Dispensation" in which the Holy Spirit is gathering out the elect (chosen) of the Church, and during which Israel is scattered among the nations. When the Present Dispensation has run its course, and the "Fullness of the Gentiles" has been gathered in along with the "remnant (remainder) according to the election of grace" of Israel, then this "Dispensation of Grace" will end, and the elect of Israel will be gathered back from the four residences of the earth to keep the Feast of Trumpets at Jerusalem. (See Romans 11:5; Matthew 24:31).

5. **The Feast of Trumpets.**

The Feast of Trumpets, which was observed on the first day of the Seventh month, ushered in the second series of the "Set Feasts." It fell on a Sabbath day, at the time of the New Moon, and ushered in the Jewish New Year. It was followed by the "Day of Atonement', on the 10th day of the month, and by the "Feast of Tabernacles" which began on the 15th day of the month, a Sabbath day, and ended on the 22nd day of the month, which was also a Sabbath day. It was ushered in with the blowing of Trumpets. During the Wilderness Wandering, two silver Trumpets made of the atonement money of the

God's Kairos Revealed

people, were blown for the *"calling of the Assembly"* and for the *"journeying of the Camps"* (See Numbers 10:1-3).

The fact that the Feast of Trumpets comes immediately at the close of the *"Interval"* between the two series of *"set feasts"* is not without significance. As we have seen the *"Interval"* represents this *"Dispensation of Grace"*, and we know that two things are to happen at the close of this Dispensation. First, the Church is to be caught out, and secondly Israel is to be gathered back to their own land.

When the Church is caught out, "For the Lord Himself shall descend from Heaven with a shout, with the voice of the Archangel, and with the Trump of God" (1 Thessalonians 4:16 KJVA), and "… We shall not all sleep (die), but we (who are then alive) shall all be changed, in a moment, in the twinkling of an eye, at the Last Trump; for the Trumpet shall sound, and the dead shall be raised incorruptible, and we shall be changed" (1 Corinthians 15:51, 15:52 KJVA).

This *"last trump"* is not the list of the *"Seven Trumpets"* that sound in the Book of Revelation, for it does not sound until the *"Middle of the Week"*, while the Church is caught out before the beginning of the week. We probably are to understand by the *"last trumpet"* the last of the Two Trumpets used by Israel, the first, for the *"calling of the Assembly"*, will call out the dead in Christ from their graves, and the second or *"last"*, for the *"journeying of the camps"*, will be the signal for the upward journey of the risen and transformed saints to meet the Lord in the air.

Then we read in Matthew 24:31, that the Son of Man, when He comes in the clouds of heaven with power and great glory at the Revelation of Himself, shall send His angels with a great sound of a Trumpet, and they shall gather together His *"elect"* (not of the Church but of Israel) from the four winds, from one end of heaven to the other. From this we see that the *"Feast of Trumpets"* has a typical relation to the *"catching out"* of the Church, and the re-gathering of Israel at the Second Coming of Christ.

6. The Day of Atonement.

The *"Day of Atonement"* was Israel's annual cleansing from sin. For a full account of the day and its services read Leviticus 16:1-3. Its typical meaning was fulfilled in Christ. He is our Great High Priest, who instead of offering a *"Sin-Offering"* for Himself, offered Himself as a *"Sin-Offering"* for us. (See Hebrews 9:11-13). But the fact that the *"Day of Atonement"* is placed between the *"Feast of Trumpets"*, which we have seen will have its typical fulfilment at the Second Coming of Christ, and the "Feast of Tabernacles", which is a type of Israel's *"Millennial Rest"*, implies that it has some typical significance between those two events. It must therefore, refer to the time when a *"... Fountain will be opened to the House of David and to the inhabitants of Jerusalem for sin and for uncleanness" (Zechariah. 13:1 NIV)*. That is, there will be a National *"Day of Atonement"* for Israel after they have been gathered back to their own land unconverted, and shall repent and turn to God. (See Zechariah 12:9-11).

7. The Feast of Tabernacles.

This was the last of the *"Seven Set Feasts"*. It was a *"Harvest Home"* celebration to be observed at the end of the harvest, and was to continue for seven days. (See Deuteronomy 16:13). The people during the Feast were to dwell in booths made of the branches of palm trees and willows from the brook, which would remind them of the palm trees of Elim, and the *"Willows"* of Babylon. (See Psalm 137:1-3). The Antitype of this Feast has not as yet appeared though Peter anticipated it, when on the Mount of Transfiguration, he said - *"Lord, it is good for us to be here; if thou wilt, let us make here three Tabernacles; one for Thee, and one for Moses, and one for Elias." (Matthew 17:4 KJV)*. Peter desired the dwelling of heavenly beings with earthly people on earth, it was not possible then, but will come to pass in Millennial Days, when Heaven and Earth shall be in closer union. The Feast of Tabernacles points forward to Israel's *"Millennial Rest"*.

What the *"Seventh Day"*, or Sabbath, is to the week, a day of rest; so the *"Seventh Month"* to the other six months of the *"Seven Month Cycle"*, typifies a period of rest - the *"Sabbatic Rest"* of the *"Millennial Age"* or 1000 years, in relation to the other six thousand years of the world's work day history. Like the Lord's Supper is to us, a *"Memorial"* pointing back to the Cross and forward to the Coming, so the *"Feast of Tabernacles"* will be a *"Memorial"*, to Israel, pointing back to Egypt and forward to the Millennial Rest.

While the Feast of Tabernacles began on the Sabbath and continued seven days, it was to be followed by a Sabbath. (See Leviticus 23:39). This Sabbath on the *"Eighth Day"* points to the New Heaven and Earth that follow the Millennium, and to the "Eighth Dispensation" the Dispensation of the *"Fullness of Times"*.

Below is the Hebrew Calendar starting with the 1st month of each year, ending with the last month of each year. This is

Watch and Pray

the calendar God's people are using. They NEVER used the Gregorian calendar.

Hebrew	English	Number	Length	Civil Equivalent
	Nissan	1	30 days	March-April
	Iyar	2	29 days	April-May
	Sivan	3	30 days	May-June
	Tammuz	4	29 days	June-July
	Av	5	30 days	July-August
	Elul	6	29 days	August-September
	Tishri	7	30 days	September-October
	Cheshvan	8	29 or 30 days	October-November
	Kislev	9	30 or 29 days	November-December
	Tevet	10	29 days	December-January
	Shevat	11	30 days	January-February
	Adar I (leap years only)	12	30 days	February-March

God's Kairos Revealed

For us to understand the times of the second return of our Messiah, we need to understand the appointed times of God as revealed to mankind. With this understanding you are able to see where we are now. And if you know where you are, it is easy to determine where you are going. It is very important for us to keep guard, for we do not know the hour. How do you keep guard of what you don't know? Knowledge is the key that God has given to mankind to open the doors of eternal life.

Watch and Pray

CHAPTER ELEVEN

YOUR APPOINTED TIME

VICTIM OF GOD'S PURPOSE

The understanding that God uses people to get His purpose accomplished on the earth could be a message you need to hear in order to understand and answer all the questions that have remained unanswered in your life. In the quest to resolve spiritual and personal struggles, explanations become a cure that somehow help us close matters. It is only human to want to know why you are going through this suffering right now, and what wrong you have done to go through the troubles you may be facing.

The reason we suffer and why we may go through what seems to be undeserved and unjustified sufferings is that we suffer because we are victims of God's purpose. God uses people to affect people. He uses people to establish people. And God has ordained that His Most Holy people go through the worst suffering in order to have His greatest purpose accomplished. You may be a victim of God's purpose if you are suffering for Christ's sake and not suffering for wrong doing. God needs to accomplish a specific purpose but He can only do it through you. If He has chosen you, then discomfort, persecution and ridicule, will be your proportion till His purpose has been fulfilled.

The life of Joseph is the most relevant example in scripture. The account in Genesis presents the life of Joseph as one with unfair treatment and undeserved jealousy from his own brothers; from his early childhood 'till thirty years of age, Joseph's life was one of rejection after rejection. As you go through this account you will begin to sympathize with Joseph for the troubles he has been through. Even Joseph himself tried to justify himself to the cupbearer about the situation he had found himself in. Regardless of his explanations and request for intervention, he didn't get the sympathy he expected because the bible records that after the cup bearer was released from prison, he forgot about Joseph.

Even when the people he helped forgot about him the bible records this: But God ... But God was with Joseph. Many times it seemed like he was all alone, in a foreign prison for something he didn't do and no way of freedom. But Jehovah Shammah was there with him. PURPOSE CAN SUSTAIN A PERSON!

The dream speaks

Joseph was sold by his brothers as a slave to the Ishmaelites, who also sold him to the Egyptian Officer Potiphar. God Almighty revealed his plan to Joseph through a dream many years earlier. In God's agenda Joseph was a saviour, but God didn't reveal to him the process and the journey. He showed him the end in the beginning. How many of us know where we should be but don't know how to get

Your Appointed Time

there? How many of us are called to be God's salvation plan to our families, communities and nations? Sometimes we faint along the way because we look at the situation, we look at the prison and forget the dream.

We do not forget only the dream; we also forget the God of the dream. Our God is a strategist. In every mess, He has a message for you, He has it all figured out. Prophet Jeremiah was imprisoned and the Word of the Lord penetrated through the prison walls to reach him. God will never forsake you in your prison or desperate time. You might be bound in your prison, but God's Word in you cannot be bound. Is anything, I mean is there anything at all too hard for God?

We later see Jacob and his children who were a total of seventy people relocating to Egypt because of famine in their land. Little did they know that it was all a heavenly setup, and God, confided in his friend Abraham about his descendants being foreigners for 400 years. The All-knowing God and Father did not tell Abraham how his descendants will get to the foreign land, He only told him that they will not end up there. Judah and his brothers did not know that when they were selling Joseph they were actually helping to fulfill that prophecy. When his brothers sold him, they thought that they got rid of the problem. Throughout this ordeal, Joseph learned that it was God's purpose for him to come to Egypt, it was for the good of his family and for the fulfilment of his dreams, hence, he did not become bitter against his brothers.

Watch and Pray

Promotion is coming your way as promised

- **From a family to a nation**

Exodus 1

Israel multiplied according to the promise God gave to Abraham. They were promoted from being a family of twelve children to a family of seventy people when they migrated to Egypt. In Egypt they multiplied from a family to a nation of over a million people. They made progress in their Egypt. You may be afflicted, but you are growing stronger and wealthier in your Egypt. You do not have to feel it to have it, just know it. The more the Egyptians afflicted them the stronger they became. But Israel did not know that she was a threat to Pharaoh, that is why they were begging Pharaoh not to afflict them with hard labour. Israel also did not know that the afflictions strengthened her. Can you relate to Israel's situation? Pharaoh confessed his fears to the Egyptians, that is why He afflicted Israel. Many times when affliction come our way, we conclude that we are afflicted because of our weaknesses and sin. The truth is, it is our strength, ability and powerful destiny that attracts and threatens the enemy. The enemy knows that if he can remind you of your sins, he will defeat you easily, as the spirit of self-condemnation will get to work to distract you. When you are feeling guilty about something, you cannot effectively pray. This becomes the foothold of the enemy to afflict you. Repentance is the key to dealing with sin and guilt. Sin should not draw you further away from God, it should rather, draw you nearer to the Father in name of Jesus Christ. His mercies are more than your sins.

Your Appointed Time

When you run away from God, you are running straight into the arms of the devil.

King David said I would rather fall into the hands of God than into the hands of my enemies, for I know He will have mercy on me.

This does not mean that God cannot punish sin. This simply means that even when God disciplines you, He will remember the blood of His son Jesus and show you His mercies.

God said to Abraham, your descendants will be foreigners for four hundred years, and we learn from the Word of God that they stayed thirty years more, which totals to four hundred and thirty years. They were comfortable in the Land of Egypt as tenants, that they forgot the promise that God made to their father, that "I will give you your own land, you are ordained and born a landlord".

Life throws challenges at us that needs us to respond to them. If we fail to respond to the challenges, we end up settling for less. We tend to settle for mortgage bonds and become tenants of the banks than trusting God to give us the ability to build our houses in our own land and become landlords.

We see Pharaoh feeling intimidated by the Israelites. He also started to strategize against them. When you are highly favoured, you become a threat to the less favoured. The enemy does not know that favour is not fair. It is not personal; it depends on who is your God, and the enemy takes your success very personal.

Watch and Pray

Pharaoh in his plan against Israel, did not plan for the unforeseen circumstance. For God is the God of the unforeseen circumstances. Israel has a God, you have a God, invisible to man, but His work is visible to all mankind. Pharaoh ill-treated the Israelites so much that they started to seek God in tears. I can relate to the Children of Israel. Often times we receive a Word of prophecy about our lives, and God does not tell us how He will fulfil that Word. When we are ill-treated, we opt to panic and lower the Power and the Ability of God to deliver us, to the level of our fears. We even plan to help God fulfil His promises. God is self-sufficient, He does not need advisors and analysts to assist Him to finish the work he had started in us.

One thing about every problem that you face, be it a sickness, virus, a marital problem, unemployment, poverty and abuse, is that "they all have an "EXPIRY DATE", attached to them".

- **He is coming to save you**

When the appointed time came, God raised Moses to deliver His people out of the land of Egypt to the Promised Land.

Let God raise your Moses today, in Jesus Mighty name, to assist your destiny and speak on your behalf, Amen.

The time of deliverance had come for Israel, but God had to fight the strongholds of Egypt first before the Israelites could be set free. Many times we feel it is time to breakthrough, but we find ourselves not prepared for battle. For any breakthrough in life, you need to be ready to fight, as the Word suggest. You need to break something or someone to get through so you can gain access. Battles and attacks are an indication that we are in God's set time. Remember child of God, it is impossible to fail because your victory was predestined.

For every birthing there are midwives

The highest level of warfare

Action attracts reaction

When God acts on your behalf, your enemies react to counteract God's action. We tend to feel the reaction mode more than the action mode.

Let us declare and say: *"From today, I refuse to act on my emotions in Jesus name, Amen".*

Emotions and feelings can be deceiving. Let us view God in Action on behalf of His people. Our focus in this context will be on the 10th plague.

The Number ten and its multiples (10, 100, 1000), often illustrates the Fullness of whatever is in view, without it necessarily being the totality, we can sum it by saying number ten symbolizes the fullness of time of whatever is in view. God dealt with the strongholds and the gods of the Egyptians from the first to the ninth plagues. On the tenth plague God had to complete His mission of deliverance in Egypt. When people lose their wealth and assets they might still counteract the action, because they know they can recover their wealth, but when people lose their children they surrender because they know they cannot replace or resurrect the dead. The enemy starts to submit to a higher power and confesses their wickedness.

When the Egyptian firstborn's died that night, the hope of the Egyptian families and their priesthood was altered forever. This time Egypt had no choice but to release God's firstborn Israel.

"And all the firstborn in the land of Egypt shall die, from the firstborn of Pharaoh that sitteth upon his throne, even unto the firstborn of the maidservant that is behind the mill; and all the firstborn of beasts" (Exodus 11:5 KJV).

"For I will pass through the land of Egypt this night, and will smite all the firstborn in the land of Egypt, both man and beast; and against all the gods of Egypt I will execute judgment: I am the LORD" (Exodus 12:12 KJV).

Recipe for victory

The main Law that determines victory in Warfare is the Law of obedience to Instructions. It is important to listen and obey the instructions from God without question. It may be instructions from God, leaders or His Prophets. Sometimes prophetic instructions sound foolish and senseless especially to logic oriented people, just obey. Once you compromise or dilute the instructions, you may end up dead or being a casualty in warfare.

"And they shall take of the blood, and strike it on the two side posts and on the upper door post of the houses, wherein they shall eat it" (Exodus 12:7 KJV).

The instructions were clear to Israel. They were expected to slaughter a lamb according to the instructions given. And

Your Appointed Time

the blood had to be applied on the door posts. When God or the Angel sees the applied blood, He would pass over them.

If Israel ignored the application of the blood of the lamb on their door posts and lintels, they would have died on that night of the Passover.

Warfare meal

Israel had to eat the flesh of the lamb roasted with fire and unleavened bread, that guaranteed them strength for the Journey, with bitter herbs that reminded them of their bitter life in Egypt. Israel had to also follow instructions on how to eat the Passover meal.

"And they shall eat the flesh in that night, roast with fire, and unleavened bread; and with bitter herbs they shall eat it. Eat not of it raw, nor sodden at all with water, but roast with fire; his head with his legs, and with the purtenance thereof" (Exodus 12:8-9 KJV).

Israel's captivity in Egypt, demonstrated how the enemy binds and imprisons the lives of people. The level of warfare that God engaged in, shows how profound God's love is towards us. Think of the plagues that God had to release to judge the gods of Egypt, but still Pharaoh was stubborn. Jehovah God had to go to the extremes and kill to set Israel free. Israel is a chosen nation to demonstrate how God deals with families, communities and nations.

The very same plagues that God released upon the enemies of Israel, He can release them on your behalf today. The same Angel of death that passed through Egypt to destroy the firstborn of the enemy, is still available to defend your

Watch and Pray

family today. All you need to do is ask the Father. He will gladly come to your rescue.

CHAPTER TWELVE

THE SHADOW ECLIPSED THE SUBSTANCE

"Question 19 in the Heidelberg Catechism says, "God began to reveal the gospel already in Paradise; later God proclaimed it by the holy patriarchs and prophets and foreshadowed it by the sacrifices and other ceremonies of the law; and finally God fulfilled it through his own beloved Son".

"For these rules are only shadows of the reality yet to come. And Christ himself is that reality" (Colossians 2:17 NLT).

Before Jesus came, God showed us His shadow first in Patriarchs, Matriarchs and their descendants after them. What does this mean?

This will take us back to some of the reasons why God created man:

- He created man that He can have the Image of Himself (physical appearance)
- God created man to fill the earth with the likeness of Himself (character, is Spiritual), God created man so that He can show forth His love.),

Watch and Pray

- He created men to procreate so that we can multiply and fill the earth.

Before Adam and Eve could sin, God knew. And this knowledge never stopped God from creating them, it rather made Him want to redeem them from their sins, by laying His own life down. God's desire to give Himself for mankind would not be possible because God is a spirit. For His plan to be possible, He needed a mortal human body through which he could suffer, bleed, and die for us, and reveal His nature of love. We see the unconditional love of God demonstrated through His giving. It is the unconditional (agape) love that gives. All other kinds of love take.

We need to understand that Jesus is God himself. He is the Word of God that became flesh and lived among men. Some times when we speak about Jesus, we tend to think of another person or prophet that God created. God did not create a son, but He begot a Son.

"For God so loved the world, that he gave his only begotten Son, that whosoever believeth in him should not perish, but have everlasting life" (John 3:16 KJV).

The term "begotten" Son refers to Jesus being God's son in the biological sense. Jesus carried the DNA of God and He was 100 % God and 100 % human. And God fathered a biological son. In all this, God was putting Himself in the position of earthly fathers. God knows how fathers (parents) feel about their children.

Let us view an example of the Substance, Jesus prefigured in Abraham's Test.

The Shadow Eclipsed the Substance

Abraham did not know that He was being tested. What He heard and knew was that he must go to the appointed place which was in the region of Moriah to give the highest form of sacrifice. HIS ONLY SON whom he loved.

"This is what God said to Abraham, "And He said, "Take now thy son, thine only son Isaac, whom thou lovest, and get thee into the land of Moriah; and offer him there for a burnt offering upon one of the mountains which I will tell thee of. And Abraham rose up early in the morning, and saddled his ass, and took two of his young men with him, and Isaac his son, and clave the wood for the burnt offering, and rose up, and went unto the place of which God had told him. Then on the third day Abraham lifted up his eyes, and saw the place afar off. And Abraham said unto his young men, Abide ye here with the ass; and I and the lad will go yonder and worship, and come again to you. And Abraham took the wood of the burnt offering, and laid it upon Isaac his son; and he took the fire in his hand, and a knife; and they went both of them together. And Isaac spake unto Abraham his father, and said, My father: and he said, Here am I, my son. And he said, Behold the fire and the wood: but where is the lamb for a burnt offering? And Abraham said, My son, God will provide himself a lamb for a burnt offering: so they went both of them together. And they came to the place which God had told him of; and Abraham built an altar there, and laid the wood in order, and bound Isaac his son, and laid him on the altar upon the wood. And Abraham stretched forth his hand, and took the knife to slay his son. And the angel of the LORD called unto him out of heaven, and said, Abraham, Abraham: and he said, Here am I. And he said, Lay not thine hand upon the lad, neither do thou anything unto him: for now I know that thou fearest God, seeing thou hast not withheld thy son, thine only son from me. And Abraham lifted up his eyes, and looked, and behold behind him a ram caught in a thicket by his horns: and Abraham went and took

the ram, and offered him up for a burnt offering instead of his son. And Abraham called the name of that place Jehovah Jireh: as it is said to this day, In the mount of the LORD it shall be seen. And the angel of the LORD called unto Abraham out of heaven the second time, and said, By myself have I sworn, saith the LORD, for because thou hast done this thing, and hast not withheld thy son, thine only son: That in blessing I will bless thee, and in multiplying I will multiply thy seed as the stars of the heaven, and as the sand which is upon the sea shore; and thy seed shall possess the gate of his enemies; And in thy seed shall all the nations of the earth be blessed; because thou hast obeyed my voice. So Abraham returned unto his young men, and they rose up and went together to Beersheba; and Abraham dwelt at Beersheba. (Genesis 22:2-19 KJV).

From the above quoted scripture, we see Isaac represented as the shadow of the Christ, the substance to come.

Notice, not any Mountain was communicated to Abraham, but a Specific Mountain. God has chosen specific Mountains for all future sacrifices. He has set aside a specific location for the redemption of mankind. There is a specified place for your miracle, breakthrough and establishment. It is not going to happen anywhere and anyhow. Our God is a God of intention and purpose. On the third day of his Journey, Abraham and Isaac arrived at Mount Moriah. And he offered up Isaac in the afternoon of the fourth day from when God had originally spoken to him, which was when he had originally set him apart to be offered up as a sacrifice unto death.

Likewise, Jesus Christ was set apart four days (4000 years) before he was offered up on Mount Golgotha.

Isaac the Son of his father Abraham is a type of Christ, *"The Son of His Father God"*. As Abraham was willing to offer

The Shadow Eclipsed the Substance

up his beloved son Isaac as a sacrifice at Mount Moriah, God also offered his only begotten Son as a sacrifice on Mount Golgotha. In doing so, their seed was greatly multiplied and blessed.

Take note of the following important similarities from the scripture above and the actual events of the cross.

The Lamb that God provided to Abraham took the place of Isaac, like Christ took my place and your place. Amen

Isaac carried the woods necessary for his own sacrifice up a lonely Mount Moriah like Jesus carried his Cross up to Golgotha.

This was, and always will be, the essential meaning of Passover. All the previous blood sacrifices even going back to the Garden of Eden looked forward to the coming of a greater and ultimate sacrificial Lamb. In His atoning blood all the previous accounts based upon faith and a blood sacrifice would be taken note of and covered. If there was faith in the heart of

Watch and Pray

the one making the sacrifice, then their sins would be accounted for, and settled.

Our father Abraham knew not about that promised Sacrificial Lamb. Abraham's willingness to do this believing God would bring life back from death, was the indispensable faith of Abraham. And this faith was necessary on his side of the covenant. The lamb with his head caught in the thicket of thorns was of course provided by God. The lamb provided for Abraham on this occasion, was a substitute for the life of his son Isaac.

We see the crucifixion drama foreshadowed in this awesome scene. Abraham's only son Isaac was submissive and humble unto death.

Isaac allowed himself to be bound by his father, like Jesus who allowed himself to be separated with his Father.

Mount Moriah was an awesome, even an awful place of slaughter. It was also the Holy Place that would bring atonement for sin. God saw faith demonstrated in the obedient actions of His covenant partner Abraham.

And so, the God of Abraham then acted powerfully on His side of the covenant on behalf of Abraham. We see the promised New Covenant fulfilment recorded in the pages of the New Testament. You are a covenant child and God's side of the covenant is a settled matter concerning you.

Though you may fail along the way, He can never change. Abraham had his shortcomings but God still called him friend. His lie did not change his status in God. So are you, all the promises that God made are still standing, do not be deceived,

The Shadow Eclipsed the Substance

He is the same Yesterday, Today and Forever. Arise and take your position. He loves you enough to forgive you. His mercies are equal to His Majesty.

Watch and Pray

CHAPTER THIRTEEN

UNDERSTANDING THE TIMES

Lack of understanding of times and seasons can cost a nation and people. Israel overstayed in Egypt, and when they begged Pharaoh about their hard work, he made things worse for them. Mothers lost their children when Moses was born. King Herod killed children that are two years and younger when Jesus Christ was born. It becomes important to understand the seasons and times concerning the matters of nations and families. When Daniel discovered that after seventy years, God promised a visitation and release from captivity. He knew what to do. He approached the throne of God in prayer and fasting on behalf of God's people and heaven invaded the earth and released the nation back to rebuild Jerusalem.

1 Chronicles 12 gives us an account of David's great army which was assembled in Hebron. We read of the thousands of warriors who came from every tribe. There were 6,800 from the tribe of Judah bearing shield and spear and from the tribe of Simeon, 7,100 mighty men of valour fit for war. The tribe of Zebulun is recorded to have 50,000 warriors who were experts in all weapons of war and who could keep ranks.

Watch and Pray

Amidst that list of thousands of mighty men, we read of the small number of chiefs from Issachar. Only 200 men, but they had understanding of the times to know what Israel ought to do. A great number of warriors is not needed for a battle if there are those who have understanding of the times and seasons. These are the ones who carry the "strategy" within them that will defeat the enemy. You need the grace to understand the times and seasons in your life and understand what to do to experience a life of results.

"And God said, let there be lights in the firmament of the heaven to divide the day from the night; and let them be for signs, and for seasons, and for days, and years:" (Genesis 1:14 KJV).

"To everything there is a season, and a time to every purpose under the heaven" (Ecclesiastes 3:1 KJV).

God created light in Genesis 1 to divide the night from the day and seasons, and for days and years. The creation of times brought about an understanding of past and future activities that take place on the earth. The introduction of time played a crucial role in the redemption plan for mankind. The church has the power to go back in time and go forward in time through prayer and correct the errors of yesteryears and release the desired future. We can command creation to cooperate with us and resist satanic instructions. We can redeem our time and command the moon, sun and stars to engage in battle in our favour. Time is created to favour us and those in control of time controls everything.

Corridors of time

Understanding the Times

- Moments can mean a very brief portion of time or exact point in time;
- Seconds,
- Minutes,
- 12 Hours a day, 12 Hours a night, 24 hours a full day,
- Watches, 4 watches day, 4 watches in the night,
- 365 DAYS a year (excluding leap year),
- 52 Weeks a year,
- 12 Months in a year,
- 4 Seasons a year, summer, winter, spring and autumn,
- Years,
- Decades 10 years,
- Generations 30 years,
- Centuries 100 years,
- Millennia 1000, and
- Eternity (Infinite Time/Endless Time After death).

"Jesus answered, Are there not twelve hours in the day? If any man walk in the day, he stumbleth not, because he seeth the light of this world" (John 11:9 KJV).

Rank's of times

1. Moments are gateways to seconds. Seconds are gateways to Minutes. The first second of the minute becomes a gate to that minute.
2. Minutes are gateways to Hours; the first minute becomes the gate to the hour.

Watch and Pray

3. Hours are gateways to Watches. The first hour becomes the gate to the watch. The first watch of the night becomes the gate for the beginning of the night.
4. Watches are gateways to Days.
5. Days are gateways to Weeks. The first day becomes the gate for the beginning of the week.
6. Weeks are gate ways to Months. The first week becomes the gate for the beginning of the new month.
7. Months are gateways to Seasons. The first month of a season becomes a gate of that season.
8. Seasons are gateways to Years. The first year becomes a gate of the decade.
9. Years are gateways to Decades. The first decade becomes the gate for the beginning of generations.
10. Decades ushers Generations. The first generation becomes the gates for the beginning of a new century.
11. Generations ushers in Centuries. The very first century becomes a gate for the beginning of a new Millennium.
12. Centuries ushers in Millennia.
13. Millennia usher in Eternity.

Importance of understanding times

"And from the sons of Issachar, men who had understanding of the times, to know what Israel ought to do, the heads of them were two hundred. And all their brothers were at their command" (1 Chronicles 12:32 KJV).

Whosoever controls the times controls everything. When you possess understanding of times, you will know what to do, how to do it and when to do it.

Understanding the Times

Lines of time

"Their line is gone out through all the earth, and their words to the end of the world. In them hath he set a tabernacle for the sun" (Psalm 19:4 KJV).

There are lines that are invisible to man's natural eye that are responsible for times and seasons on the earth. These are called imaginary lines. They have both natural and spiritual meaning. These lines can utter speech and people have influence over these lines of times and seasons.

These imaginary lines are known as:

Latitude: these are access points which run from the east to west.

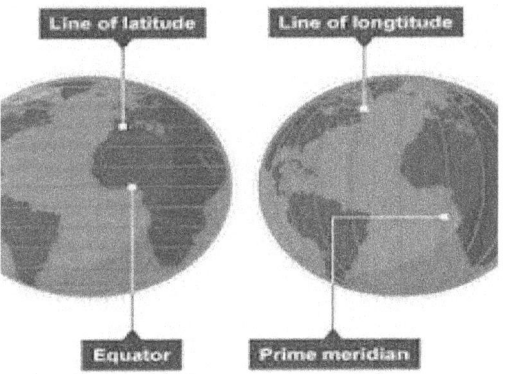

- These lines vary in length and the longest of them is the Equator which is called the Latitude Zero (0).
- The Horizontal lines are in charge of the Gates of seasons such as Summer, Winter, Autumn and Spring.

Watch and Pray

- They are also ports for spiritual season as programmed in the spirit such as seasons of promotion, peace, breakthrough, and harvest.

LONGITUDE: These are Access Points: which run from the north to south pole.

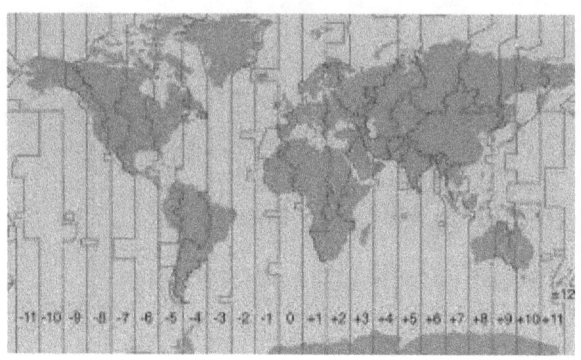

- They are Vertical lines in charge of the Gates of time.
- These lines are equal in length to each other.
- The furthest point from Longitude Zero to the East and West is 180 degrees.

Crossing/Intersection point

The point of intersection between the Equator and Greenwich Meridian is in the Atlantic Ocean. People use the power of creation to take advantage of the weak and unknowing. Intersection points have a spiritual meaning in the prophetic sphere. One can create collisions at intersection points that can actually materialise in the lives of people. We need to understand that the word accidents does not exist in the spirit. Everything happening in our lives is intentional. The enemy creates the pain, and what we call accidents.

Understanding the Times

Begin to pray against the creation of the enemy and the gathering of the wicked at intersection points.

I declare that all witches and satanic agents that use these lines of time to fly for my sake, when they reach the point of intersection at the Atlantic Ocean, may the lines reject them and the sea swallow them in Jesus Mighty name. Amen.

Prophetic action and prophetic praying can reverse the actions of the wicked. You possess the power to trample upon serpents and scorpions and all powers of the enemy.

"For the king of Babylon stood at the parting of the way, at the head of the two ways, to use divination: he made his arrows bright, he consulted with images, he looked in the liver" (Ezekiel 21:21 ASV).

"There shall not be found among you anyone who makes his son or his daughter to pass through the fire, or a fortune-teller, soothsayer, omen reader, or sorcerer, or one who cast spells, or a medium, a spiritist, or one who calls up the dead. For whoever does these things is an abomination to Adonai, and because of these abominations Adonai your God is driving them out from before you. You are to be blameless before Adonai your God. "For these nations, which you are about to dispossess, listen to soothsayers and fortune-tellers, but as for you, Adonai your God will not allow you to do so. "Adonai your God will raise up for you a prophet like me from your midst-from your brother" (Deuteronomy 18:10-15 TLV).

Drive or walk to the Crossroad near you, begin to fire from your life, office and land all the people consulting diviners, observers of clouds, witches, fortune tellers for your sake in Jesus name. Amen.

Watch and Pray

At the crossroads one needs to decide to either go on straight or turn to the left or right. Destiny diverters stand at the cross roads to send your life to the wrong direction. By the time you realise that you are lost, you are already forty years old, married to a wrong woman or man, with five children and even employed by a wrong company. It is important for us to deal with witches working against our lives. If you do not deal with them, they will certainly deal with you. God declared that these practices are an abomination before Him. God announced that He will drive them out of the land before the very eyes of Israel.

"Thou shalt not suffer a witch to live" (Exodus 22:18 KJV).

Refuse to share your wealth with evil doers. Declare that every promotion intended for you must have your name engraved on it. Anyone who plans to dethrone you from your God given position, we stand in agreement at the crossroad and we send them to a wrong direction, in Jesus name. Refuse to be defeated by the wicked in Jesus name. God further said, we must remain perfect before him, we should not be tempted to use the services of the people consulting the dead, diviners, observes of the clouds, witches and sangomas. It is totally forbidden by God.

I declare that all the doers of evil in my land and destiny, be fired in Jesus name.

I dominate my environment and I possess my inheritance in Jesus name. Amen.

Understanding the Times

Why did the king of Babylon choose an intersection point to perform divination?

Crossroads or intersection points are powerful gates. Cross roads have a four way stop, meaning they allow or deny you access to a road at a certain point.

If you are a slow driver, you might not get access to the road at the time you are supposed to. Imagine if the king programmed confusion upon the drivers at the intersection point of two national roads. What can you expect? Have you ever seen an accident on a stop street? Many times, the victims cannot even explain what really happened? They do happen a lot, not because they are meant to happen. Somebody is using divination at the right place to cause confusion, blindness and accidents.

Declare:

- Arise and declare that any divination used against my life at the parting of ways, to confuse my life and destiny I send you back to eat your senders.
- Any idols consulted to bring my life down, fall down and die in Jesus name.
- Any arrow sent against my life at the intersection point, to frustrate my life and cause me to take a wrong direction, I send you back to pierce your senders in Jesus name.
- I receive the Power of Jesus to function effectively at the partying of ways. Amen.

Watch and Pray

CHAPTER FOURTEEN

POWER OF ATTRACTION

The earth and the moon rotate around a star named Sol, which is known as the "Sun", one of over 100 billion stars in the Milky Way. The moon is mentioned 62 times in scripture, and it is the earth's satellite, and revolves around the earth. Genesis 1:14-18 declares; and God said; let there be lights in the firmament of the heaven to divide the day from the night; and let them be for signs, and for seasons, and for days, and years: and let them be for lights in the firmament of the heaven to give light upon the earth: and it was so. And God made two great lights; the greater light which is the sun to rule the day, and the lesser light which is moon to rule the night: he made the stars also. And God set them in the firmament of the heaven to give light upon the earth, and to rule over the day and over the night, and to divide the light from darkness: and God saw it was good. And the evening and morning were the fourth day.

Psalm 136:8-9 The sun to rule by day: for his mercy endure forever, the moon and stars to rule by night: for his mercy endures forever. By day the sun shines without competing with the moon and stars, by night the sun withdraws itself and the

Watch and Pray

moon and starts shine and show different phases and dimensions of glory. By day the moon and stars withholds their splendour for they know when to shine and for what purpose.

A ruler is a person exercising governance or dominion, others say a ruler is a king, queen, or a supreme leader, a person who has a supreme power or authority.

The sun, moon and stars are given supreme power and authority to govern the night and day. They are not human king or queen but they understand power, governance, authority and dominion. The bible further declares that they are created to divide the day from the night. No one will come and say, oh sun it is time to go, its night now, the sun has that understanding of governance same as the moon and the stars. The meticulous flow between these elements and the order they display make people want to worship them because they carry so much power and they command authority. People need to understand that the sun, moon and stars are created for the people, they are created to serve the earth, not for the earth or people to serve them.

I would like us to focus on the government and power of the moon and the impact this element has on people.

There are eight phases of the Moon, but in this Chapter our focus will be on the four moon phases and the impact they have on us.

Power of Attraction

Phases of the moon – lunar phases

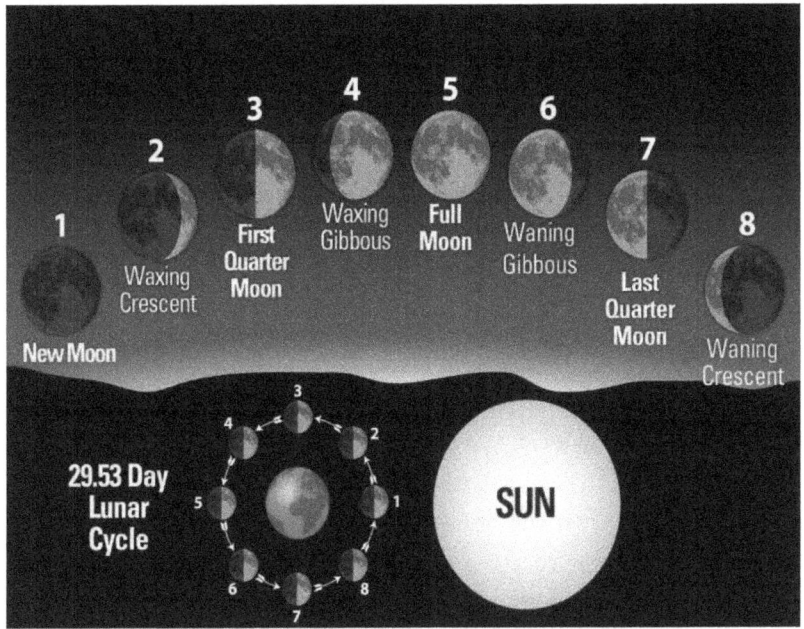

IPTC photo Metadata – Mila Gligoric – Fitolia

The reflection of the sun on the moon, determines the different lunar phases as viewed on the earth. The moon travels towards the east among the stars and makes a complete circle each month. It orbits the earth once every 27.322 days and it takes approximately 27 days for the moon to rotate once on its axis.

We can associate the moon and its phases to the life of a believer. Your life as the moon is depending on the reflection of the sun of Righteousness which is Jesus Christ to shine and manifest positive phases and seasons in your life. The attraction of the sun towards the moon as the earth rotates determines what the moon will release to the earth.

Creation in general has an influence on life and God has made us to be gods on the earth and govern with him. He gave us dominion over the fish of the sea which is the marine realm, and over the fowl of the air which is the air realm, and over everything that moves upon the earth which is the land realm.

There are people who understand and have studied the elements and they know the power they carry. Some of them take advantage of these powers and use them to afflict and control the lives of others. It is very important to empower yourself with knowledge so that you can defend yourself from the enemy's control. He uses the very same creation that God has created to serve us, to abuse us. Satan and his agents do not have their own creation; they do not have their own human beings to use. They use the very same creation of God to afflict people who are supposed to be beneficiaries of this creation.

Did you know that the moon influences everything under the sun?

"Woe to you experts in the law, because you have taken away the key to knowledge. You yourselves have not entered, and you have hindered those who were entering." (Luke 11:52 NIV).

1. The Impact of the new moon

It is the first phase of the moon and it lasts more or less three and half days. The new moon season is regarded as a time of new beginnings, fresh starts, optimism, hope, joy and the resurrection of faith.

Power of Attraction

This is also the time of celebration, feasting and programming your life in prayer and giving praise to God.

1.1 Time to sound the Trumpet before the Lord and Feast

"From one New Moon to another and from one Sabbath to another, all mankind will come and bow down before me," says the LORD" (Isaiah 66:23 NIV).

1.2 Time of open door of Heavenly Temple and Courts

"This is what the Sovereign LORD says: The gate of the inner court facing east is to be shut on the six working days, but on the Sabbath day and on the day of the New Moon it is to be opened" (Ezekiel 46:1 NIV).

1.3 Time of Worship

"On the Sabbaths and New Moons the people of the land are to worship in the presence of the LORD at the entrance to that gateway" (Ezekiel 46:3 NIV).

1.4 Time of God's judgement

If you are disobedient to God the enemy can use this time of the new moon to programme affliction so that you be devoured during the new moon celebrations. *"They are unfaithful to the LORD; they give birth to illegitimate children. Now their New Moon festivals will devour them and their fields"* (Hosea 5:7).

1.5 Time of giving your offering to the Lord

"On the day of the New Moon he is to offer a young bull, six lambs and a ram, all without defect" (Ezekiel 46:6 NIV).

Watch and Pray

The New Moon symbolizes the time in a month whereby you are given an opportunity to celebrate in worship, programme new things in your life and receive revival. Record new moon season per month on your diary and tap into the benefits that God has bestowed into the new moon. Command the new moon to release new things for your life, church and nation.

2. Waxing Moon (starts as crescent to first quarter, then waxing)

It is the season whereby the moon increase in apparent size. It becomes larger and stronger.

Declare during this time that your life is emerging and growing stronger and better. During this moon phase, it is also time to grow and build your spiritual life. Your prayer life becomes stronger during this lunar phase.

Draw up your plans and present them before God in PRAYER

3. Full Moon (from waxing to full moon)

"Sound the Ram's horn at the New Moon, and when the moon is full, on the day of our Feast" (Psalm 81:3 NIV).

It is the time of abundance, renewing of covenants and vows, harvest, achieving dreams and praying for protection for yourself and loved ones. The moon is releasing so *much power and the enemy and satanic agents, witches and workers of iniquity uses this time of the full moon to renew their covenant* by drinking human blood and programming afflictions, diseases, poverty, divorces,

Power of Attraction

debts and division of the church against believers and the nations of the world.

3.1. The Full Moon Phase is Time to push in prayer especially at midnight

- This is not the time for the church to sleep; it is time to take over the cities, families and your possessions.
- It is also a time of prophetic utterances, engaging in spiritual warfare and tapping into the power the full moon has and silence the pulling of the moon that has been programed by the enemy against the lives of believers.
- The full moon season is like an open door of heaven. The womb of the moon is ready and open to conceive that which will be declared and programmed for the next cycle. Creation is groaning for the revelation of the sons of God. Because the power that God gave to the moon to rule the night was meant to compliment the believers but the enemy uses it to afflict them.
- This is also time to wage war in praise and worship and experience the foundations of your prison opening up, chains falling and doors opening up for your family, church and nation.

3.2. Here is a list of some of the Full Moon's effects on humans that have been documented.

- Hospital accident and emergency units see about 10% more patients.
- Significant increase in visits to medical practices for consultations after the full moon.

Watch and Pray

- Increase in epileptic seizures, bleeding ulcers, and intensive period pains for women.
- Dramatic rise in admissions to psychiatric hospitals.
- Higher number of mental patients become highly disturbed.
- The Full Moon adversely affects patient behaviour.
- Airline passengers create more incidents.
- Crimes of violence increase in the full moon season.
- Murders, many apparently motiveless increase three times more during this phase.
- Arson attacks increase by 100%.
- Suicide rates increase.
- Alcohol consumption rises at the start and end of the lunar cycle.
- More drunk drivers, more crashes and more hangovers.
- Ovulation — and sexual desire — peak with the Full Moon.
- Emotional imbalance increases during the full moon and arguments in marriages, relationship, and unnecessary short temper and irritation manifests.

Let God arise and release every member of your family who is affected negatively by the lunar powers in Jesus Mighty name. Every evildoer who has programmed madness, divorce, miscarriage, and confusion against your family, we send the incantation back to sender in Jesus name.

Power of Attraction

Declaration by faith

Oh you moon, Elohim is your creator and He is my Heavenly Father, therefore, release my family, I command you in the name of Jesus Christ to go and smite and silence my enemies this full moon in Jesus name. Psalm 121:6 declares; the sun shall not smite me by day, nor the moon by night. Every opposition using the sun and the moon to smite me, I resist you by the word of God. I render you powerless. The sun, moon and stars will cooperate with me as they fought from heaven, the stars in their courses fought against Sisera to favour Deborah and her army (See Judges 5:20).

4. **Waning Moon** (the moon decreases from full moon to *waning gibbous phase*, and is reduced to a *crescent phase*, and the cycle goes back again to new moon. During the waning phase the moon is decreasing in apparent size. This is the time of clearing away, cleansing, releasing, shedding old patterns and opening up to the Lord.

Pray and declare that as the moon is waning away, the *problems in your life are also fading with the moon.*

The Sun, Moon and Stars mark the times and seasons in the natural. This elements mark also, spiritual seasons. It could mark seasons of positive and negative manifestation, such as seasons of favour, grace, abundance, famine, death, sickness and disgrace in a person's life.

The moon influences and controls women's pregnancies and menstrual cycles. The moon also pulls the minds of people; hence we have lunatics. The witches, magicians and palm readers use the strength of the moon to flow and programme confusion, get things they didn't work for, bewitch, afflict, and programme madness in the lives of their targets.

Arise in Prayer and confront the enemy during the lunar cycles and refuse to be a target in Jesus name. The enemy shall eat their own flesh and be drunk from their own blood.

"And I will feed them that oppress thee with their own flesh; and they shall be drunken with their own blood, as with sweet wine: and all flesh shall know that I the LORD am thy Saviour and thy Redeemer, the mighty One of Jacob." (Isaiah 49:26 KJV).

"Violence shall no more be heard in thy land, wasting nor destruction within thy borders; but thou shalt call thy walls Salvation, and thy gates Praise. The sun shall be no more thy light by day; neither for brightness shall the moon give light unto thee: but the LORD shall be unto thee an everlasting light, and thy God thy glory. Thy sun shall no more go down; neither shall thy moon withdraw itself: for the LORD shall be thine everlasting light, and the days of thy mourning shall be ended" (Isaiah 60:18-20 KJV).

Shalom!

CHAPTER FIFTEEN

THE DUAL OFFICES OF THE MESSIAH

Politics and Religion can never be separated. The power struggle in the world today is as a result of political and religious reasons, more than it is personal or family reasons. Jesus Christ presides over both the Political office as a King and the Priestly office as the High Priest, after the order of Melchizedek.

"For this Melchizedek, king of Salem, priest of the Most High God, who met Abraham returning from the slaughter of the kings, and blessed him" (Hebrews 7:1 KJV).

We see the same offices manifested in the life of Melchizedek the King of Salem and the High Priest of the Most High God. We see also the manifestation of Jesus' Priestly ministry at His first coming as the Lamb of God ready to be offered at the altar of the Cross.

Jesus's death and resurrection made us Kings and Priests unto God. We possess the dual anointing as priests unto God and we are Kings and Governors over our situations.

Watch and Pray

Our Kingly Offices

- As a King you dominate your environment.
- You do not rule over physical people but over spirits and situations.
- You must rule and dominate on the earth. In heaven the King (God) of Kings (me and you) is already there, ruling and reigning. You cannot rule in heaven.
- Your domain is the earth realm; in heaven we will be submitting to the authority of our King.

Our Priestly Offices

- And as a Priest, you minister before God the Father, through praise and worship.
- You also offer sacrifices of praise and worship to Him.
- You stand in the gap on behalf of others. Never under estimate your ministry as a priest on earth. Excel in your priestly office, direct destinies of your children and all those God has entrusted you with.

"And hath made us kings and priests to God and his Father; to him be glory and dominion for ever and ever. Amen" (Revelation 1:6 KJV).

Jesus' Ministry as High Priest was fulfilled before Crucifixion

When the High Priest tore his Clothes, in Mathew 26:65 before crucifixion, he was actually officiating the ministry of Jesus Christ as the High Priest.

The Dual Offices of the Messiah

"Then the high priest rent his clothes, saying, He hath spoken blasphemy; what further need have we of witnesses? Behold, now ye have heard his blasphemy" (Matthew 26:65 KJV).

Two Offices after the Order of Melchizedek

Melchizedek is the High Priest of God Most High. He is also King of Salem, (Jerusalem) (See Psalm 110:4).

Political role

On Jesus' second coming, He will appear in His Political and Kingly role. He will not appear as a suffering servant and Lamb as His first appearance was, He will return as a conquering King. The trumpets will sound and declare the commencement of the last days.

The nations are increasingly raging against the coming of the Messiah. Jesus Christ will return just in the incision of time; before godless humanistic rule threatens to completely destroy all life on earth.

"I will surely assemble, O Jacob, all of thee; I will surely gather the remnant of Israel; I will put them together as the sheep of Bozrah, as a flock in the midst of their pasture; they shall make great noise by reason of the multitude of men. The breaker is gone up before them: they have broken forth and passed on to the gate, and are gone out thereat; and their king is passed on before them, and Jehovah at the head of them" (Micah 2:12-13 KJV).

As the 70th week ends, He will return to His Holy City. Right there, and at that time, the trampling of Jerusalem will cease. Jesus Christ will come as a deliver and Conquering King, riding upon a white horse. At the ends of the earth the Messiah

Watch and Pray

will come bringing deliverance to His hard pressed people. The Breaker will come to the Sheepfolds of Bozrah, at Jerusalem, the Lion of the tribe of Judah will roar from Zion. (See Joel 3:16). He will bring the sceptre of His righteous rule to this earth. The long expected Son of David will come at last. And He will rule from David's Throne.

"And the angel said to her, Fear not, Mary: for thou hast found favour with God. And behold, thou shalt conceive in thy womb, and bring forth a son, and shalt call his name JESUS. He will be great, and will be called the Son of the Highest; and the Lord God will give to him the throne of his father David. And he will reign over the house of Jacob for ever, and of his kingdom there will be no end" (Luke 1:30-33 DARBY).

In that magnificent future Millennium of Messiah, Jerusalem will finally become the "City of Peace". The nations will find Salvation under Messiah's glorious ministry and rule. And this poor ruined creation will again be restored to the beauty and order it once knew.

We are ordained kings and priests unto our God, our Father. Let us take our position as kings and issue decrees concerning our lives, our families and our nations. Let us take over the gates, market place and our streets in Jesus name.

CHAPTER SIXTEEN

KNOWLEDGE IS A KEY

"And the key of the house of David will I lay upon his shoulder; so he shall open, and none shall shut; and he shall shut, and none shall open" (Isaiah 22:22).

"In the beginning God created the heavens and the earth. And God called the light, Day. And He called the darkness, Night. And the evening and the morning were the first day. And God called the expanse, Heavens. And the evening and the morning were the second day" (Genesis 1:1, 5, 8 ASV).

In the beginning God did not name days of the week. Monday, Tuesday, Wednesday, Thursday, Friday, Saturday and Sunday He called them First, Second, Third, Fourth, Fifth, Sixth and Seventh day. He only gave the authority of naming animals to Adam. There is no record in scriptures where God said to Adam name animals, days and months.

Someone made history by changing the heavenly order of God for days by giving them names of stars, planets or gods of this world etc. and further changed the day of worship which is Sabbath to Sunday. I do not have a problem with men's awesome pro-activeness to be innovative and bringing about

Watch and Pray

change; my concern is the origin of these names. What is the spirit behind these names, what is the impact of this change when it comes to keeping track of the time of the return of Messiah and Sabbath rest and worship? What impact do these names have on our everyday life? As we say we watch and we pray, do we have knowledge of these planets and the spirit behind those names?

Look at this scripture...

"My people are destroyed for lack of knowledge: because thou hast rejected knowledge, I will also reject thee, that thou shalt be no priest to me: seeing thou hast forgotten the law of thy God, I will also forget thy children" (Hosea 4:6 ASV).

The scripture above shows clearly the consequences of ignorance or failure to acquire knowledge. It is the responsibility of every one of us to seek knowledge and understanding. If you do not seek knowledge, the enemy will bring to you his version of knowledge, and he can make you accept and believe his lies. The Holy Spirit is God in our Midst. He is our counsellor, and He will guide us to all the truth. Revelations and Knowledge is God's desire for you. Let us pursue knowledge.

The Naming of the Days

The Greeks named the days of the week after the sun, the moon and the five known planets, which were in turn named after the gods Ares, Hermes, Zeus, Aphrodite, and Cronus. The Greeks also called the days of the week the Theon hemerai "days of the gods". The Romans substituted their

Knowledge is a Key

equivalent gods for the Greek gods, Mars, Mercury, Jove (Jupiter), Venus, and Saturn.

The Germanic peoples generally substituted roughly similar gods for the Roman gods, Tiu (Twia), Woden, Thor, Freya (Fria), but did not substitute Saturn.

Below is a table divided into four columns. The first two shows the names of the days of the week in English and their meaning. The third and fourth shows the Hebrew name and meaning.

Secular Weekday Name	Meaning Planet and Personality	Hebrew name	Original Meaning
Sunday Genesis 1 named this day first day – people changed it to Sun-day	Day of the sun The professed Christians in Alexandria and Rome did not keep the Biblical Sabbath. Instead they started keeping Sunday in honour of some ancient tradition over bible truth. Sun worship and Christian ran parallel.	Yom Reeshone	1st day
Monday	Moon day Moon as a god and	Yom shaynee	2nd day

Watch and Pray

Secular Weekday Name	Meaning Planet and Personality	Hebrew name	Original Meaning
	ancient people used to worship the moon.		
Tuesday	Germanic god of war and sky equated to the Roman god of Mars.	Yom Shlee´shee	3rd day
Wednesday	Roman god of commerce, travel, thievery, eloquence and science Messenger of other gods	Yom Revee´ee	4th day
Thursday	*"Thunder's day"* Jupiter (Jove) is the supreme Roman god and patron of the Roman state. He is noted for creating thunder and lightning.	Yom Khah´mee´shee	5th day
Friday	Freya (Fria) is the Teutonic goddess of love, beauty, and fecundity	Yom Ha´shee´shee	6th day

Knowledge is a Key

Secular Weekday Name	Meaning Planet and Personality	Hebrew name	Original Meaning
	(prolific procreation). She is identified with the Norse god Freya.		
Saturday	Saturn is the Roman and Italic god of agriculture He is believed to have ruled the earth during an age of happiness and virtue.	Shabbat (Rest)	7th day

You may be asking this question, what do I do now with this knowledge?

It may not help considering to change a calendar now, begin to dethrone every heavenly personality enthroned upon your days. Declare that the spirits of these personalities will not rule your life.

"Hast thou commanded the morning since thy days; and caused the dayspring to know his place; that it might take hold of the ends of the earth, that the wicked might be shaken out of it?" (Job 38:12-13 KJV).

- Begin to pray and shake off the influence of innovation of the enemy over your life in Jesus name.

Watch and Pray

- Speak to the morning to hold the earth by its edges and let it begin to shake out every evil programming and planting of the enemy over your destiny.

"The heavens declare the glory of God; and the firmament sheweth his handywork. Day unto day uttereth speech, and night unto night sheweth knowledge. There is no speech nor language, where their voice is not heard" (Psalm 19:1-3 KJV).

Whether we feel it or not, the devil is using people to get his agenda established on earth. If the naming of days was not important to the devil, it would still be called day 1, day 2 and so on. The enemy brought about change so that we can miss the time of God's visitation. No wonder the church even worships on Sunday and not on Sabbath. Enthrone Jesus as King and Lord over your days, weeks and years.

Understand that days, weeks, months, years and seasons, are all gates. The function of a gate is to allow and deny access. If the church does not guard its gates, it becomes vulnerable to the attacks of the enemy.

"And I say also unto thee, that thou art Peter, and upon this rock I will build my church; and the gates of hell shall not prevail against it" (Matthew 16:18 KJV).

From the scripture above, Jesus was saying to Peter, upon this revealed knowledge, I will build my Church, and the Gates of hell shall not prevail against it. Furthermore, gates have powers to fight and prevail against people.

"Lift up your heads, O ye gates; and be ye lift up, ye everlasting doors; and the King of glory shall come in. Who is this King of glory? The LORD strong and mighty, the LORD mighty in battle. Lift up your

Knowledge is a Key

heads, O ye gates; even lift them up, ye everlasting doors; and the King of glory shall come in" (Psalm 24:7-9 KJV).

Gates can speak, and can also resist men. Like traffic robots denying you access when they turn red. Remember, somebody is in charge of robots. There are also spiritual traffic robots that are programmed to deny people access to promotion and progress in life. Miracles are like opportunities; you act and grab them as they present themselves. If you cannot discern the opportunities and miracles, you will miss your moment.

Once you miss an opportunity, your life might never be the same again. Every second counts. It is said that a change in 1 degree on the rotation of the earth which is equivalent to four minutes of time can cause life to cease. Imagine that, a change of four minutes causes life to cease what more a full hour?

After crucifixion Jesus was disfigured and the Gates could not recognize him. He had to command the gates to lift up their heads. Time is a gate; whosoever controls the gates is in charge of everything. If the god enthroned on the gates of your life is a god of war, it means you must contend for your life. And if you are not a fighting type, then what? You will end up settling for less. The devil is not stupid; he has put systems in place to keep his hands on your inheritance. You need to acquire as much knowledge as possible and apply it through prayer for your benefit and the benefit of your country, family and church.

Watch and Pray

CHAPTER SEVENTEEN

WHY DO WE USE THE ANOITING OIL?

We use the anointing oil for:

- For establishing and sealing of covenants, and
- Anointing of the sick.
- Raising of Altars as instructed by the Holy spirit.
- House cleansing and consecration.
- Setting things apart.
- Ordaining leaders.

The New Testament clearly states that anointing oil should be a part of the church's ministry to the sick.

"Is any one of you sick? He should call the elders (spiritual leaders) of the church to pray over him and anoint him with oil in the name of the Lord" (James 5:14 AMP).

The book of Mark 6:13 tells us that the disciples of Jesus anointed the sick with oil. They drove out demons and anointed sick people with oil and healed them.

Watch and Pray

Whatever our reasons for anointing with oil, it is important to understand that there are no magical properties in the anointing oil. When we anoint, we are simply exercising faith in obedience to His Word. The supernatural part is left entirely up to God.

We also use the Anointing oil:

To consecrate a person, object or location to God.

"I washed you in water. Yes, I thoroughly washed away your blood from you, and I anointed you with oil" (Ezekiel 16: 9 WEB).

Webster's definition of the word consecrate is *"to devote irrevocably to the worship of God."*

God instructed Moses to consecrate the Tabernacle, its utensils and the Priests by anointing them with oil (See Exodus 40:9-11, 13,15).

Practical examples: today it might include a church, a home or even a musical instrument which is used for worship.

As believers, we are living Temples or Tabernacles (1 Corinthians 6:19) through Jesus Christ, and we too can use our bodies and our possessions to honour or dishonour God. By anointing them, we set them apart to serve God and not evil.

- To Rededicate yourself after the fall

"So David arose from the ground, washed and anointed himself ..." (2 Samuel 12: 20 NKJV.)

Why Do we Use the Anointing Oil

What is the Anointing?

The anointing is the extraordinary power of God, to make things happen. We can name the anointing in this context "the I CAN SIDE OF GOD".

How can I use the Anointing oil in spiritual warfare?

- Prior to going into battle and for protection

    "Prepare the table, set a watchman in the tower, eat and drink. Arise princes, anoint the shield" (Isaiah 21: 5 NKJV).

    Throughout Bible times, people, places and objects have all been anointed with oil.

Where can I use the Anointing oil?

- People - family members, ministry workers, friends etc.
- Buildings: before you lay a foundation for a house, anoint the land and declare that you will finish building. Invite the trinity of God. Pray and redeem the land also.
- You can also anoint the existing Property, and destroy the spirits that were occupying the property before you occupied it.
- Places of worship to set it apart for God's work.
- Offices: anoint your office, place of work and invite the presence of God. Declare that all evil programming against your joy, progress at work will not prevail in Jesus name.
- Possessions: Bed and Pillows: You can anoint your bed and pillows and rebuke the spirit of being bed ridden. It is upon this altar that witches and assailants come,

when you are defenceless and half dead. Declare also dreams of destiny not nightmares.
- Drive out spirit beings such as spiritual husbands and wives that are unauthorized to visit you. If you are married, declare the faithfulness and joy in your marriage.
- Vehicles: Declare no accidents and ask God to assign Angels to look after your cars and worship God with your possessions.

James 5:14 makes it clear that when we anoint with oil, we must do so in the name of the Lord. As believers, we express the name of the Lord in the three persons of the Trinity - the Father, the Son and the Holy Spirit.

How can I use Anointing oil in my family, marriage and home?

- Marriage and family is the first ministry that God ordained in the Garden of Eden, and it is also the first ministry that the enemy attacked.

It is very important to pray for your marriage. Establish a family altar of prayer as a couple, and the husband being the authority of the house should speak over the wife's life and womb, declaring her fruitfulness and rebuking the spirit of barrenness from her life. Isaac's prayer for Rebecca dealt with the spirit of barrenness and released twins representing double portion of a blessing. What a prayer, imagine if husbands can begin to pray and anoint their wives? Breakthrough is guaranteed. Barrenness from work, finances, and other areas of your life cannot withstand the prayer of the husband.

Why Do we Use the Anointing Oil

Sometimes we seek help outside our home, while your help is right under your roof.

"Isaac's wife could not have children. "Isaac prayed to the LORD for her. The LORD heard Isaac's prayer, and He allowed Rebekah to become pregnant" (Genesis 25:21 ERV).

It is important for the husband to direct his family's spiritual life. The father is the authority of the house, and God expects fathers to account for the wellbeing of their families. Adam was busy in the garden and he did not realize that entertaining his hectic schedule was a crack (door way) on the hedge of protection over his family. The serpent is always waiting outside the hedge of every home, to enter so he can kill and destroy. Many infidelities that occur in families come as a result of a crack that will soon be an open door.

God has put a hedge of protection around our families. And the responsibility lies with us to ensure that the devil has no access into our homes.

"Hast not thou made an hedge about him, and about his house, and about all that he hath on every side? Thou hast blessed the work of his hands, and his substance is increased in the land" (Job 1:10 KJV).

If you break a hedge that God puts over your life, the serpent will enter and bite you. Families realize through pain that the serpent is in the house.

"... and whoso breaketh an hedge, a serpent shall bite him" (Ecclesiastes 10:8 KJV).

Watch and Pray

Pray with your children

It is important for parents to pray and anoint their children with oil and declare the protection and the purpose of God for their lives to prevail. Fight for your children's destinies in Prayer. Refuse the devil access into their lives. Imagine if your parents knew what you know today, and prayed for you from the time when you were still in the womb. Imagine if your parents prayed about the name they gave you, imagine if God approved your name, I am not talking about a grandmother's/grandfather's name that some people inherited. Imagine if your parents gave you an offering and taught you to tithe from childhood. Imagine if your parents taught you God's Word and prayed with you from Childhood, imagine how your life would be today.

You can develop a culture of anointing your children weekly or monthly and declare the protection of God upon their lives. If we do not pray for our children and teach them how to pray, media, satanic agents, and their peers at school will teach and influence them.

Lot and his wife did not teach their children about the fear of the Lord. Sodom and Gomorrah influenced and taught them how to solve problems the Sodom's way. Sodom and Gomorrah was burnt to ashes, but its teachings had already made an impact in the lives of Lot's daughters. We see in Genesis after they evacuated Sodom, along the way the wife became the pillar of salt, the daughters caused their father to drink too much alcohol and they had intercourse with him.

Why Do we Use the Anointing Oil

And they begat children, by their father. Can you imagine their sons were their half-brothers? This was an abomination before God.

"And the firstborn said unto the younger, our father is old, and there is not a man in the earth to come in unto us after the manner of all the earth. Come, let us make our father drink wine, and we will lie with him, that we may preserve the seed of our father. And they made their father drink wine that night: and the firstborn went in, and lay with her father; and he perceived not when she lay down, nor when she arose. And it came to pass on the morrow, that the firstborn said unto the younger, Behold, I lay yester night with my father: let us make him drink wine this night also; and go thou in, and lie with him, that we may preserve seed of our father" (Gen 19:31-33 KJV).

Who can use the Anointing oil?

Below is some guidance of who can use the anointing oil according to scriptures.

- **Every disciple of Jesus** - *"And they cast out many demons, and anointed with oil many who were sick, and healed them" (Mark 6:13 JUB).*
- **Elders/leaders of the church** - *"Is anyone among you sick? Let him call for the elders of the church, and let them pray over him, anointing him with oil in the name of the Lord" (James 5:14 NKJV).*
- **Repentant sinners** - *"And behold, a woman in the city who was a sinner, when she knew that Jesus sat at the table in the Pharisee's house, brought an alabaster flask of fragrant oil, and stood at his feet behind him weeping; and she began to wash his feet with her tears, and wiped them with the hair of her head; and*

Watch and Pray

she kissed his feet and anointed them with the fragrant oil" (Luke 7:37-38 NKJV).

As believers, we may even anoint ourselves - *"So David arose from the ground, washed and anointed himself, and changed his clothes; and he went into the house of the Lord and worshipped" (2 Samuel 12:20).*

Watch and Pray

PRAYER WATCH

SECTION C:

UNDERSTANDING THE TIMES OF PRAYER AND PROGRAMMING PRAYER WATCH

The Bible teaches and instructs believers to stay awake physically, to pray and also to watch spiritually in prayer to avoid the snares that lead to temptation. The scripture speaks of prayer watches which are precise times of the day and night on which we can pray. The prayer watch consists of four watches a day and four watches a night that cover 24 hours a day.

For heaven to invade the earth with miracles and solutions men ought to pray always and not faint.

"Jesus returned to His three disciples. Now they were sleeping. He said to Peter, "Simon, you are asleep! You could not stay awake even for even one hour! You must keep awake and you must pray. Then you will not to do something wrong. You really want to do the right thing, but your body is week" (Mark 14:37-38).

Watch and Pray

What is to Watch?

To watch means to look out, to see an approaching danger and warn those who are endangered.

It is during the watch that God gives us solutions and ways that nullify the trusted weapons of the enemy. When we see the nation under attack, it is time for us to watch and become more vigilant. When Jesus was on earth, He separated himself to pray and kept watch and warned his disciples to do the same. 1 Thessalonians 5:6 declares, "Therefore let us not sleep, as do others; but let us watch and be sober."

In this book we will start with the evening watches that cover the twelve hours of the night and end with the day watches that covers the twelve hours of the day.

Summary of the Night Watches

1. The First watch of the Night: 18:00 – 21:00

- This is the time to pray and silence all the voices of the enemies on our life, family, church, city and nation.

2. The Second watch of the Night: 21:00-00:00

Time for divine favour. (Exo.3:21-22, 11:3-4, 12:35-36, Psalm 5:12; 45:12; Esther 2:9, 15, 17) This is the time to receive your provision or supply (strength, abilities, freedom from all limitations, etc.).

Pray for Divine Protection. (Psalm 3:1-7; 17:8-14, Acts 23:23; Zech. 1:10).

3. The Third watch of the Night: The Midnight Warfare Watch 00:00-03:00

Why Do we Use the Anointing Oil

Time for spiritual warfare. This is time when the deep sleep falls upon men according to Acts 20:7-12. Remember, according to Matthew 13:25.

4. The Fourth Watch of the Night: The Morning Watch: 03:00-06:00

This is a time for divine judgements.

Summary of the Day watches

1. The First Watch of the Day: 06:00-09:00

A time where divinity meets humanity, at sunrise

This is also the time for the outpouring of the Holy Spirit for Equipping for the Market place, Service and for our Light to Shine in this day. (2 Cor. 9:3; Acts 1:8; Isa. 60:1-22; Matt. 5:16)

2. The Second Watch of the Day: 09:00-12:00

This is a time of forgiveness and healing of relationships

3. The Third Watch of the Day: 12:00-15:00

This is the hour of crucifixion – Mark 15:25 declares, *"And it was the third hour, and they crucified him, and the superscription of accusation was written over, THE KING OF THE JEWS"*.

4. The Fourth Watch of the Day: 15:00-18:00

The transformation watch, the veil in the temple was rent into two, from top to bottom Matthew 27:45-53.

Time to gain access to places where we were denied before.

Time of the covering to be removed and receive a clear vision.

Watch and Pray

PRAYER WATCH

CHAPTER EIGHTEEN

NIGHT WATCHES

THE FIRST NIGHT WATCH
18H00-21H00

The Watch that terminates the Day and Ushers in the night. It is an Altar where people meet God Face to Face.

The hour of worship

"My soul shall be satisfied as with marrow and fatness; and my mouth shall praise thee with joyful lips. When I remember thee upon my bed, and meditate on thee in the night watches" (Psalm 63:5).

"In the tabernacle of the congregation without the veil, which is before the testimony, Aaron and his sons shall order it from evening to morning before the LORD: it shall be a statute for ever unto their generations on the behalf of the children of Israel" (Exodus 27:21 KJV).

Watch and Pray

"You will bring them in and plant them on your own mountain, the place, O LORD, which you have made for your abode, the sanctuary, O Lord, which your hands have established" (Exodus 15:17 KJV).

"Mine eyes prevent the night watches, that I might meditate in thy word" (Psalm 119:148 KJV).

The hour to stand in the gap for our children (salvation of others)

"Their heart cried unto the Lord, O wall of the daughter of Zion, let tears run down like a river day and night: give thyself no rest; let not the apple of thine eye cease. Arise, cry out in the night: in the beginning of the watches pour out thine heart like water before the face of the Lord: lift up thy hands toward him for the life of thy young children, that faint for hunger in the top of every street" (Lamentations 2:18-19 KJV).

"For a thousand years in thy sight are but as yesterday when it is past, and as a watch in the night" (Psalm 90:4 KJV).

This is the time for divine beginnings:

Evening time came before morning. This watch marks the beginning of the new day. It is a connection point between day and night. It is the first watch of the 24 hours period. Many times night season come before morning season in our lives, careers, callings and destiny. We should rejoice because the night season ushers in the morning season.

"For his anger endureth but a moment; in his favour is life: weeping may endure for a night, but joy cometh in the morning" (Psalm 30:5 KJV).

"And God called the light Day, and the darkness he called Night. And the evening and the morning were the first day" (Genesis 1:5 KJV)..

Night Watches

The hour to bury the dead in preparation to start over

"But when David saw that his servants whispered, David perceived that the child was dead: Therefore David said unto his servants, is the child dead? And they said, he is dead. Then David arose from the earth, and washed, and anointed himself, and changed his apparel, and came into the house of the LORD, and worshipped: then he came to his own house; and when he required, they set bread before him, and he did eat. And David comforted Bathsheba his wife, and went in unto her, and lay with her: and she bare a son, and he called his name Solomon and the LORD loved him" (2 Samuel 12:19-24 KJV).

- It is also a time to bury the dead Issues of the day before you worship God. David buried his child whom was conceived in sin and went to the house of the Lord to worship. And God comforted both of them and Solomon was born after their loss and pain.
- Something Good is about to come out of your loss, failures, pain and your discouragement if you know what to do when you experience pain, loss and disappointments. Some people go to consult from evil altars and bring more misfortune in their family because of pain.

This is also the hour of worship and sacrifice (evening sacrifice)

We see from the scripture below where a rich man offered the highest form of worship at the evening Watch.

- *"When the evening was come, there came a rich man of Arimathaea, named Joseph, who also himself, was Jesus' disciple. He went to Pilate, and begged the body of Jesus. Then Pilate commanded the body to be delivered. And when Joseph had taken the body, he wrapped it in a clean linen cloth, and laid it in his own new tomb, which he had hewn out in the rock, and he rolled a great stone to the door of the sepulchre, and departed" (Matthew 27:57-60 KJV).*

- *"And it came to pass at the time of the offering of the evening sacrifice, that Elijah the prophet came near, and said, LORD God of Abraham, Isaac, and of Israel, let it be known this day that thou art God in Israel, and that I am thy servant, and that I have done all these things at thy word" (1 Kings 18:36 KJV).*

The manifestation of the Fatherhood of God

Jesus said in Matthew 16:16-19 that the thing we must possess are the gates, and one of the keys we need to possess is the key of the knowledge of time. Our day has a gate, our week has a gate, our month has a gate, and our year has a gate. We must possess these gates, because whoever possesses the gates controls everything. The very first watch is the gate for the beginning of the new day.

SECOND WATCH OF THE NIGHT – 21H00 - 00:00

(See Revelations 9:16; Acts 23:23; Exo. 3:21; 11:3, 4; 12:35, 36; Psalm 119:148)

Time to hallow and exalt the name of the Lord.
Time of prayer for ministries.

"Arise, and let us go by night, and let us destroy her palaces" (Jeremiah 6:5 NKJV).

"And I will give this people favour in the sight of the Egyptians, and it shall come to pass, that, when ye go, ye shall not go empty". (Exodus 3:21 KJV).

"For thou, LORD, wilt bless the righteous; with favour wilt thou compass him as with a shield" (Psalm 5:12 KJV).

- **Time for divine favour and wealth transfer.**
- This is the time to receive your provision or supply (strength, abilities, freedom from all limitations, etc.).
- The second watch of the night is also the time for plundering your oppressors.
- This is the ordained time of favour from men; time for respect from men. If you read Exodus 3:21- 22; 11:3-4; 12:35-36; you will see that God made the Egyptians favourably disposed towards the Israelites, so that the Egyptians gave Israel whatever they asked for.

Watch and Pray

- In Acts 23:23, we see Paul enjoying favour from the captain of the soldiers during this same period.

"And the LORD gave the people favour in the sight of the Egyptians. Moreover, the man Moses was very great in the land of Egypt, in the sight of Pharaoh's servants, and in the sight of the people. And Moses said, thus saith the LORD, at about midnight will I go out into the midst of Egypt" (Exodus 11:3-4 KJV).

"And, the maiden pleased him, and she obtained kindness of him; and he speedily gave her things for purification, with such things as belonged to her, and seven maidens, which were meet to be given her, out of the king's house; and he preferred her and her maids unto the best place of the house of the women" (Esther 2:9 KJV).

- Pray against temptation: Jesus came and asked Peter. He said, "Rise, and let us go for my betrayer is at hand." This period is the time to pray for strength against all temptation and trials.

3. **Pray for Divine Protection.** (See Psalm 3:1-7; 17:8-14, Acts 23:23; Zechariah 1:10). This is also the period to pray and ask for the release of the armies of God to give angelic escort (See Zechariah 1:10, Acts 9:23). We see in Acts 23:23, the same army General that had arrested Paul, now ended up protecting Paul! As you pray today; pray that God will cause the people who have worked against you before to protect His purpose in your life. What the governor could not enjoy was given to Paul as he was given 470 Roman Soldiers as escorts. So every provision we need to do God's work will be released at this time. (See Acts 23:23-53).

4. **Prayer for Provision to do God's Work.** (See Exodus 11:3-4). Time for the Supply of all Resources needed for every God-given project. (See Exodus 35 36 and compare with 12:35, 36). Pray for the Provision. It was the time that the Israelites got everything that they had to use to build the Tabernacle in the wilderness.

THE MIDNIGHT WATCH
(00:00 MN – 3.00 AM)

"Let My People Go"

In scripture we learn that many Patriarchs faced battles and won them at Midnight. We also learn that at midnight there are many spiritual activities and battles that believers go through. Midnight is an exit gate from the night into the morning.

"For I will pass through the land of Egypt this night, and will smite all the firstborn in the land of Egypt both man and beast; and against all the gods of Egypt I will execute judgment: I AM THE LORD" (Exodus12:12 KJV).

"And at midnight Paul and Silas prayed, and sang praises unto God: and the prisoners heard them. And suddenly there was a great earthquake, so that the foundations of the prison were shaken: and immediately all the doors were opened, and every one's bands were loosed." (Acts 16:25 – 26 KJV).

- Midnight is a time for slaughter; when the destroying angel goes through the camp, community, city, or nation (See Exodus 12:29 cf. 2 Kings 19:35)
- This is a time to declare the Psalm of protection before you engage in warfare, Psalm 91:5, 6 for Divine Protection for yourself, family, church, city and nation.

Night Watches

- This a time of release from every Prison (Isa. 42:22; Jud. 16:3; Acts 16:25; Psa. 18:27-28; 2 Kings 19:35)
- This is also the time people are generally released. According to the scriptures, God released the people of Israel to leave Egypt at this time.
- It was also midnight that Samson according to Judges 16:3-4 carried the gates of the city and went out.
- This is the time the wicked are wiped out. (See Mark 1:35; Isaiah 17:14).
- This is also the time for angelic intervention.
- This is also the time you can deploy the land to fight for you. This is the time to rule in the midst of your enemies.
- This is the time of Freedom for His Bride. (Exodus 12:29; Judges 19:25) especially those who are trusting God for their marriage partners. For those who are married too, this is the best time to pray for your marriage. According to Matthew 25:6, it was at midnight that the Bridegroom came. In the case of Ruth, though she had been sleeping at Boaz's feet, it was at midnight that he noticed that a woman was sleeping there. You can pray that God will cause the Body of Christ, single ladies or men to be noticed at this time. Pray for God to show you things to make your marriage a happy one (See Ruth 3:1-10). Pray also for the discovery of new and beautiful things in your spouse.
- This period is also the time to keep the lamps burning. This watch is also the time to enter your rest (See Psalm 67).

Watch and Pray

- Best time to make your case in prayer. (See Mark 13:35; Luke 11:5-13; Acts 16:25-34; Acts 20:7-12)
- This is also the period to pray for every emergency provision God makes to be released (See Luke 11:5-13; Acts 16:3).
- It is also time of visitation through dreams (See Job 4:13-14).
- Time for miracles or covenants to manifest.
- Time for the applied Blood of Jesus to be seen and prevail.
- This is the time to awake out of sleep and confront every storm of destruction and distraction, turbulence and confusion.
- An hour of victory in battle through praise and worship.

"The LORD is a man of war; the LORD is his name" (Exodus 15:3 KJV).

"And from the days of John the Baptist until now the kingdom of heaven suffers violence, and violent men seize it" (Matthew 11:12 - EMT).

"And from the days of John the Baptist until now the kingdom of heaven suffereth violence, and the violent take it by force" (Matthew 11:12 KJV)

The time for spiritual warfare

- **SPIRITUAL** means that the battle has to do with spirits. It is fought by spirits and mainly takes place in the realms and domains of operation of spirits.
- **WARFARE** means an on-going war between two or more entities.

Night Watches

Genesis 1:26-28 states the intention of God for creating men. The fall of Lucifer from heaven marked the beginning of Spiritual Warfare. Satan, the former Archangel has intentions to destroy mankind. Satan knows nothing about love, he deceives the agents he recruits to his Occult and kingdom. He uses men to destroy others.

He uses his influence to torment, capture and frustrate the destinies of men. Fear not, the power of the cross is stronger than that of the enemy.

The mission of the devil is:

- To take as many people as possible to hell.
- He knows how much God loves people, so he thinks God cannot stand to watch people being sent to hell, so Satan is hoping that God will change His verdict about hell for the sake of people.

Let us Read this scripture,

We live in this world, but we don't fight our battles in the same way the world does.

"The weapons we use are not human ones. Our weapons have power from God and can destroy the enemy's strong places. We destroy people's arguments, and we tear down every proud idea that raises itself against the knowledge of God. We also capture every thought and make it give up and obey Christ" (2 Corinthians 10:3-5 ERV).

"Put on the whole armor of God, that you may be able to stand against the schemes of the devil. For we do not wrestle against flesh and blood, but against the rulers, against the authorities, against the cosmic powers over

this present darkness, against the spiritual forces of evil in the heavenly places" (Ephesians 6:11-12 ESV).

This is the Time of Visitation and Peculiarity

Midnight is a dangerous and a powerful gate, especially if its full moon. This is the Hour of heavenly Visitation. This time God visit the gods of the land to execute judgment.

- This is time of deliverance from bondage, an hour of breakthrough. This is the powerful hour to see God as the man of war. He distinguishes Himself from all other men made gods. Every Pharaoh, Satan, Dagon and Baal must prove to be god.
- Only the blood of Jesus can speak and save those who belong to God.

"And Moses said, Thus saith the LORD, About midnight will I go out into the midst of Egypt: And all the firstborn in the land of Egypt shall die, from the firstborn of Pharaoh that sitteth upon his throne, even unto the firstborn of the maidservant that is behind the mill; and all the firstborn of beasts" (Exodus 11:4-5 KJV).

"For I will pass through the land of Egypt this night, and will smite all the firstborn in the land of Egypt, both man and beast; and against all the gods of Egypt I will execute judgment: I am the LORD. And the blood shall be to you for a token upon the houses where ye are: and when I see the blood, I will pass over you, and the plague shall not be upon you to destroy you, when I smite the land of Egypt" (Exodus 12:12-13 KJV).

Night Watches

Look at the Manifested presence of God demonstrated below. These are the results of what happened during the hour of visitation in Land of the Philistines. This is not a social visit but a disapproving visitation. Dagon was knocked down ten nil in his own territory not just his territory but his temple, his stronghold.

"But when they rose early on the next morning, behold, Dagon had fallen face downward on the ground before the ark of the LORD, and the head of Dagon and both his hands were lying cut off on the threshold. Only the trunk of Dagon was left to him. The hand of the LORD was heavy against the people of Ashdod, and he terrified and afflicted them with tumours, both Ashdod and its territory. And when the men of Ashdod saw how things were, they said, "The ark of the God of Israel must not remain with us, for his hand is hard against us and against Dagon our god" (1 Samuel 5:4-7 KJV).

"They sent therefore and gathered together all the lords of the Philistines and said, "Send away the ark of the God of Israel, and let it return to its own place, that it may not kill us and our people." For there was a deathly panic throughout the whole city. The hand of God was very heavy there" (1 Samuel 5:11 KJV).

I announce in Jesus Name that when your enemies wake up the next morning, they will find signs of Divine Visitation. Someone greater than Dagon was present, we see the report of His visitation.

- Pray and ask God to visit your life, family, church, community, country and continent, and judge all the strange gods tormenting and delaying your life and destiny. This is the hour, do not let it pass by.

Watch and Pray

- Pray and apply the blood of Jesus over all our possessions, your family and your destiny.

The time of weeping and bereavement in the camp of the enemy

All the families of the Egyptians lost their firstborns, for some it was their only child. Priests of the families were killed that night.

They lost their wealth, Gold, Silver and precious possessions that the Israelites collected before departure.

- Unstoppable weeping and pain visited Egypt.

Declare the fate of the Egyptian's upon your enemies.

The hour of restoration and wealth transfer

- God rescued his firstborn Israel.
- They were rewarded double for their trouble – they got the silver and gold.
- They were enslaved, but at this hour, they became wealthy and even had the materials to build the house of the Lord in the wilderness.

"They said, "If you send away the ark of the God of Israel, do not send it empty, but by all means return him a guilt offering. Then you will be healed, and it will be known to you why his hand does not turn away from you" (1 Samuel 6:3 ESV).

The enemy will not release you empty handed, the wealth of your enemies will be transferred to you in Jesus name. Amen.

Night Watches

Goliath did not know he was used to fulfil the prophetic utterances. At times the enemies are used as subjects to fulfil Gods Prophetic Agenda. Look at Goliath Proud utterance. "I am Goliath the Philistine of Gath, who killed the two sons of Eli, Hophni and Phinehas the priests; Goliath thought he did something new in Israel, while he was actually used to fulfil the prophecy. God did not want an Israelite to kill Eli's family and Goliath was a perfect man for the Job. (See 1 Samuel 17:8).

"And the LORD said to Samuel, Behold, I will do a thing in Israel, at which both the ears of every one that heareth it shall tingle. In that day I will perform against Eli all things which I have spoken concerning his house: when I begin, I will also make an end. For I have told him that I will judge his house for ever for the iniquity which he knoweth; because his sons made themselves vile, and he restrained them not. And therefore I have sworn unto the house of Eli, that the iniquity of Eli's house shall not be purged with sacrifice nor offering for ever" (1 Samuel 3:11-14 KJV).

This is a special time for divine government

Set aside and cancel human decrees (see Exodus 12-14)

- Pray against the spirit of exchange at midnight

The devil is a thief, he exchanges all the dreams of God given destiny and replaces them with dreams of failure, loss and defeat. He wants you to believe that you do not deserve anything good, and you do not even dream at all. He puts a hedge of limitation in your spiritual life, breakout in Jesus' name. Bring your case to the heavenly court before the Supreme Judge and He will rule in your favour. Jesus is the

Watch and Pray

prosecutor (even interceding for you), and the Holy Spirit is your lawyer (He speaks on your behalf).

"And this woman's child died in the night; because she overlaid it. And she arose at midnight, and took my son from beside me, while thine handmaid slept, and laid it in her bosom, and laid her dead child in my bosom. And when I rose in the morning to give my child suck, behold, it was dead: but when I had considered it in the morning, behold, it was not my son, which I did bear" (1 Kings 3:19-21 KJV).

Time of Release from every Prison. (See Isaiah 42:22; Jude 16:3; Acts 16:25; Psalm 18:27-28; 2 Kings 19:35).

"And Pharaoh rose up in the night, he, and all his servants, and all the Egyptians; and there was a great cry in Egypt; for there was not a house where there was not one dead. And he called for Moses and Aaron by night, and said, rise up, and get you forth from among my people, both ye and the children of Israel; and go, serve the LORD, as ye have said" (Exodus 12:30-31 KJV).

Samson according to Judges 16:3-4 carried the gates of the enemy and went out at midnight. Arise at midnight and takeover the gates of your enemies and of cities. You are a king in your city and whatever you say becomes Law.

The time to release your marriage partner and pray for your marriage.

- *"And at midnight there was a cry made, Behold, the bridegroom cometh; go ye out to meet him" (Matthew 25:6 KJV).*

Do you trust God for a marriage partner? Pray and deal with the spirit of delay and the spiritual husbands or wives that might be occupying and delaying your marital life.

Night Watches

This is the best time to pray for your marriage. And come against the spirit of divorce and disagreements in your marriage. According to Matthew 25:6, it was at midnight that the Bridegroom came.

Pray that God will cause you to be noticed at this time and find favour. Let God open your eyes to see and know what to do to make your marriage work. (See Ruth 3:1-10, Psalm 67).

Pray against abusers and evil systems at this hour

"But the men would not hearken to him: so the man took his concubine, and brought her forth unto them; and they knew her, and abused her all the night until the morning: and when the day began to spring, they let her go" (Judge 19:25 KJV).

Best time to make your case in prayer and lift the records of your enemies before God and declare judgement. Remember our God is a Fair Judge. (See Mark 13:35; Luke 11:5-13; Acts 16:25-34; Acts 20:7-12).

Knock without fainting in your emergency hour

"And He said to them, "Which of you shall have a friend and shall go to him in the middle of the night and say, Friend, lend me three loaves of bread" (Luke 11:5 KJVA).

"And he from within shall answer and say, Trouble me not: the door is now shut, and my children are with me in bed; I cannot rise and give thee" (Luke 11:7 KJVA).

- The key to access that which is denied, is persistence in Prayer.

Watch and Pray

"I tell you that even if he will not rise and give him the loaves because he is his friend, at any rate because of his persistency he will rouse himself and give him as many as he requires" (Luke 11:8 KJVA).

- Best time to make your personal request: Against impossibility and resistance. Do not fail to keep on knocking through Prayer.

"So I say to you, Ask, and what you ask for it will be given to you; seek, and you shall find; knock, and it will be opened to you" (Luke 11:9 NIV).

Midnight is a perfect time to declare shalom to every storm in your life, Ministry and business.

Midnight hour is time to judge witches in line with the word of God *"You shall not allow a sorceress to live"* (Exodus 22:18 WEBBE).

EARLY MORNING WATCH
(3.00 AM-6.00 AM)

"And it came to pass, that in the morning watch the LORD looked unto the host of the Egyptians through the pillar of fire and of the cloud, and troubled the host of the Egyptians" (Exodus 14:24 KJV).

- The lord delivered the Israelites permanently.
- The Lord overthrew the Egyptians and drowned them into the red sea. (See Exodus 15).

Hour of revelation

Your enemies are about to discover who you are, and who your God is, and will fear you and your God.

"And the Egyptians shall know that I am the LORD, when I have gotten me honour upon Pharaoh, upon his chariots, and upon his horsemen. And the angel of God, which went before the camp of Israel, removed and went behind them; and the pillar of the cloud went from before their face, and stood behind them: And it came between the camp of the Egyptians and the camp of Israel; and it was a cloud and darkness to them, but it gave light by night to these: so that the one came not near the other all the night" (Exodus 14:18-20 KJV).

Watch and Pray

Hour of uncommon breakthrough

Where you did not know how you cross your Red Sea, your God deployed the East wind to blow with so much might that the sea could not stand against the Israelites but give way. He will surprise you, just trust and obey Him.

"And Moses stretched out his hand over the sea; and the LORD caused the sea to go back by a strong east wind all that night, and made the sea dry land, and the waters were divided" (Exodus 14:21 KJV).

He is making a way for you, sing a new song unto the Lord your God.

"And the children of Israel went into the midst of the sea upon the dry ground: and the waters were a wall unto them on their right hand, and on their left" (Exodus 14:22 KJV).

The hour of trouble upon your enemies

"And the Egyptians pursued, and went in after them to the midst of the sea, even all Pharaoh's horses, his chariots, and his horsemen. And it came to pass, that in the morning watch the LORD looked unto the host of the Egyptians through the pillar of fire and of the cloud, and troubled the host of the Egyptians" (Exodus 14:23-24 KJV).

The hour to witness the down fall of your strongmen and judgement

- The Egyptians experience a breakdown with their transport. The wheels are out, they are still driving forward pursuing you, but this time they are driving with great difficulty. The enemy will not stop trying you. It is okay, for storms to come your way. How will you know Him as the healer if you were never sick? How will you know Him as God your Peace if you were never in the storms? How can you know Him as a shepherd if you never walked through the valley of the shadow of death? All these things happen to introduce the other sides of God that you never experienced before.

"And took off their chariot wheels, that they drave them heavily: so that the Egyptians said, let us flee from the face of Israel; for the LORD fighteth for them against the Egyptians. And the LORD said unto Moses, Stretch out thine hand over the sea, that the waters may come again upon the Egyptians, upon their chariots, and upon their horsemen" (Exodus 14:25-26 KJV).

The hour of burial of the Egyptians armies

"And Moses stretched forth his hand over the sea, and the sea returned to his strength when the morning appeared; and the Egyptians fled against it; and the LORD overthrew the Egyptians in the midst of the sea. And the waters returned, and covered the chariots, and the horsemen, and all the host of Pharaoh that came into the sea after them; there remained not so much as one of them" (Exodus 14:27-28 KJV).

The hour of salvation and deliverance

"And Moses said unto the people, Fear ye not, stand still, and see the salvation of the LORD, which he will shew to you today: for the Egyptians whom ye have seen today, ye shall see them again no more for ever" (Exodus 14:13 KJV).

"I have set watchmen upon thy walls, O Jerusalem, which shall never hold their peace day nor night: ye that make mention of the LORD, keep not silence, and give him no rest, till he establish, and till he make Jerusalem a praise in the earth" (Isaiah 62:6-7 KJV).

Watch and Pray

"And they rose early in the morning and went out into the wilderness of Tekoa. And when they went out, Jehoshaphat stood and said, "Hear me, Judah and inhabitants of Jerusalem! Believe in the LORD your God, and you will be established; believe his prophets, and you will succeed" (2 Chronicles 20:20 KJV).

"Let the stars of that night be darkened; let it remain dark, and not come into light; and let it not see the morning star arise" (Job 3:9 KJV).

"For thou, O Lord, wilt light my lamp: my God, thou wilt lighten my darkness" (Psalm 18:28 KJV).

A time to praise God for the mighty breakthrough He has given you

"In the greatness of your majesty you overthrow your adversaries; you send out your fury; it consumes them like stubble. At the blast of your nostrils the waters piled up; the floods stood up in a heap; the deeps congealed in the heart of the sea. The enemy said, 'I will pursue, I will overtake, I will divide the spoil, my desire shall have its fill of them. I will draw my sword; my hand shall destroy them.' You blew with your wind; the sea covered them; they sank like lead in the mighty waters. "Who is like you, O LORD, among the gods? Who is like you, majestic in holiness, awesome in glorious deeds, doing wonders? You stretched out your right hand; the earth swallowed them" (Exodus 15:7-12 KJV).

- The day spring begins to shake everything out during this watch of the morning.
- Satanic agents return to their homes after their night activities. Attack them and frustrate their programming,

Day Watches

and declare that the day spring should shake them out of your day. (See Job 38:13).

- No spirit is supposed to remain in this state by daybreak, we see this demonstrated by Jacob's encounter with the Angel of the Lord in Genesis 32:24-30.
- Time also for the declaration of God's Word. "Thou shalt also decree a thing, and it shall be established unto thee: and the light shall shine upon thy ways" (Job 22:28 KJV).
- This is the time to Rise and Shine, for Resurrection. This is also the time when Jesus came walking on the water to release the disciples from the storms. This is the time to ask the new day to speak into your life according to God's will.
- This is also the time for resurrection power. This is the time the stone in front of the tomb of Jesus was rolled away. Every reproach must be rolled away. God says He has a covenant with the day and also with the night.

"And in the fourth watch of the night Jesus went unto them, walking on the sea. And when the disciples saw him walking on the sea, they were troubled, saying, it is a spirit; and they cried out for fear. But straightway Jesus spake unto them, saying, Be of good cheer; it is I; be not afraid" (Matthew 14:25-27 KJV).

"Day unto day uttereth speech, and night unto night sheweth knowledge" (Psalm 19:2 KJV).

Watch and Pray

CHAPTER NINETEEN

DAY WATCHES

THE FIRST WATCH OF THE DAY
(6.00 AM - 9.00 AM) 3rd hour
(See Acts 2:15; Proverbs 4:16)

The outpouring of the Holy Spirit (See Acts 2:1-4, 17)

This is the first watch of the day. This is the watch for the beginning of sunrise.

Let Jesus the sun of righteousness rise over your life and your affairs. Declare that the sun is rising with healing in its wings, healing of your prayer life, healing of relationships, healing of the soul. And shake out every programming of the enemy over your day, and enthrone Jesus over everything that concerns you. (See Acts 2:15; Psalm 2:7-9).

Watch and Pray

This is the time for the outpouring of the Holy Spirit for Equipping for Service.

- *"And it shall come to pass afterward, that I will pour out my spirit upon all flesh; and your sons and your daughters shall prophesy, your old men shall dream dreams, your young men shall see visions: And also upon the servants and upon the handmaids in those days will I pour out my spirit. And I will shew wonders in the heavens and in the earth, blood, and fire, and pillars of smoke" (Joel 2:28-30 NKJV).*

It was between 6:00 am and 9:00 am when the Holy Spirit came. (See 2 Cor. 9:3; Acts 1:8; Isa. 60:1-22; Matt. 5:16)

God gives the necessary equipment. As you step out, ask God for equipment for the day, "Give us this day…"

Receive physical strength to work and spiritual strength to pray and discern.

"O LORD, be gracious unto us; we have waited for thee: be thou their arm every morning, our salvation also in the time of trouble" (Isaiah 33:2 KJV).

- Tap into the mercies of God

"This I recall to my mind, therefore have I hope. It is of the LORD'S mercies that we are not consumed, because his compassions fail not. They are new every morning: great is thy faithfulness. The LORD is my portion, saith my soul; therefore will I hope in him" (Lamentations 3:21-24 KJV).

SECOND WATCH OF THE DAY
(9.00 AM-12.00 Noon)
1 Kings 18, 8:56; Jos. 23:14; Matt. 20:3; Acts 2:15, Gal. 2:20; Col. 3:5

The time to refuse to be idle and engage yourself in something

Ask the master to hire you in His vineyard

"For the kingdom of heaven is like unto a man that is an householder, which went out early in the morning to hire labourers into his vineyard. And when he had agreed with the labourers for a penny a day, he sent them into his vineyard. And he went out about the third hour, and saw others standing idle in the marketplace, and said unto them; Go ye also into the vineyard, and whatsoever is right I will give you. And they went their way. Again he went out about the sixth and ninth hour, and did likewise. And about the eleventh hour he went out, and found others standing idle, and saith unto them, why stand ye here all the day idle? They say unto him, because no man hath hired us. He saith unto them, Go ye also into the vineyard; and whatsoever is right, that shall ye receive. So when even was come, the lord of the vineyard saith unto his steward, Call the labourers, and give them their hire, beginning from the last unto the first. And when they came that were hired about the eleventh hour, they received every man a penny. But when the first came, they supposed that they should have received more; and they likewise received every man a penny. And when they had received it, they murmured against the good

Watch and Pray

man of the house, saying, these last have wrought but one hour, and thou hast made them equal unto us, which have borne the burden and heat of the day. But he answered one of them, and said, Friend, I do thee no wrong: didst not thou agree with me for a penny?" (Matthew 20:1-13 KJV).

Prayer points

- Refuse to be idle in Jesus Name.
- Reject evil competition, jealousy and selfishness.
- *Declare* equal and exceeding privileges with those who were called first, and those who were called at the 6th or 11th hour.
- This parable also reveals that God is debtor to no man, and that many who begin last, and promised little in religion, God can bless them with a great deal of knowledge, grace, and usefulness in His Kingdom.
- Declare that you will Preach the Word as it is, you will not withhold the truth or dilute the truth
- Declare that the recompense of reward will be given to you, but not according to the time of your conversion. Remember the declaration that the last shall be first, and the first last.
- Ask God to hire you in His Kingdom. Until we are hired into the service of God, we are standing all the day in idle. Do not be satisfied by being hired by the market-place which is the world.

Release your reward and come against the spirit of delay in your life and family.

Day Watches

Do not feel left out, you are part of the bigger picture

- Some were sent into the vineyard at the eleventh hour; but nobody had hired them before. The Gentiles came in at the eleventh hour; the gospel had not been preached to them before. Jesus is showing us that the conditions of service are the same.

Pray for the heart to celebrate others successes so that you can be celebrated in due time

- If God gives grace to others, it is kindness to them, and no injustice to us.
- See here the nature of envy. It is an evil eye, which is displeased at the good of others, and desires their hurt. It is a grief to ourselves, displeasing to God, and hurtful to our neighbours: it is a sin that has neither pleasure, profit, nor honour.
- Let us give up every proud claim, and seek for salvation as a free gift. Let us never envy or grudge, but rejoice and praise God for his mercy to others as well as to ourselves.

Refuse to be like the elder brother in the book of Luke. The return of his prodigal brother made him furious. He allowed competition, jealousy, and selfishness to stain the good he has done without knowing what is in the Fathers Will. He did not know that all that the father has was His. He did not wait for the Father to finish the sentence. Often times pain leads us to make unnecessary conclusions, and by the time we discover the truth, we already wasted galloons of tears and the blood pressure has reached the skies.

Watch and Pray

Today, let us pray and say, *"God, give me your heart; give me the grace to relax and know that you are in control".*

1. Time for Harvest.
   - This is the time to expect the manifestation of God's promises for your life (See 2 Samuel 7:25-29).
   - Receive a new heart, increase and fruitfulness.

"Then they that gladly received his word were baptized: and the same day there were added unto them about three thousand souls" (Act 2:41 KJV).

"And now, O LORD God, the word that thou hast spoken concerning thy servant, and concerning his house, establish it for ever, and do as thou hast said" (2 Samuel 7:25 KJV).

"Then will I sprinkle clean water upon you, and ye shall be clean: from all your filthiness, and from all your idols, will I cleanse you. A new heart also will I give you, and a new spirit will I put within you: and I will take away the stony heart out of your flesh, and I will give you a heart of flesh. And I will put my spirit within you, and cause you to walk in my statutes, and ye shall keep my judgments, and do them. (Ezekiel 36:25-27 KJV).

1. **Pray and declare the personality and the finished works of the Cross upon your life.**
   - Declare the Restoration of abundant life, healing, forgiveness and favour upon your life in Jesus name.
   - Jesus was crucified at the third hour (See Mark 15:25, Matthew 27:45). After having been on the cross for three hours, darkness came upon the face of the earth. Declare these benefits of the cross upon your life today.

Day Watches

Seven Bleeding Areas of Our Lord

1. **HANDS:** He was nailed on his hands. And the blood that came out of his hands speaks of the Blessings in everything that we touch. Everything that we touch shall be preserved. Nothing that goes through your hands will die. Some people who have experienced misfortune, shall be preserved by reason of shaking hands with you.
    a. Hands speak of success in business. The Word of God declares He will bless the work of your hands.
    b. If you are selling or rendering services, by the Power of the blood that came out of Jesus's hands your business is blessed and the work of your hands shall increase.
2. **FEET:** He was nailed on his feet. The blood that came out of his feet speaks of our destiny that is restored in Christ Jesus. Some places where our feet take us to are demonic places, some roads we walk on are cursed, and witchcraft traps were set, but because of the blood that came out of Jesus's feet, we are redeemed from all kinds of curses and planting of the enemy. If your feet are attacked, you cannot move. Therefore, your destiny is imprisoned. Speak to your feet that they will not carry you to wrong places at the wrong time in Jesus name.

3. **BEARDS:** speaks of favour & maturity
    a. Psalm 133:2 - It is like the precious ointment upon the head, that ran down upon the beard, even Aaron's beard: that went down to the skirts of his garments;

b. The blood that came out of Jesus's beards speaks of Spiritual maturity and Favour of God and men. Declare maturity upon the church and its elders. Pray for the spirit of son-ship. Programme the season of Favour in your life and Ministry in Jesus name.

4. **HEAD:** The blood that came out of His head speaks of Royalty and Kingship. The crown of thorns that was put on Jesus' head speaks of restoration from the fall of Adam. Adam lost his position as a god over the earth domain, and Jesus came to restore our dual offices of Kings and Priests unto God.
    a. He was wounded on the head as a result of the repeated beatings by a reed and the blood that that came out speaks of deliverance from evil thoughts, attacks and imaginations that comes through the mind.
    b. Struggles with your mind and studies are defeated by the blood that came out of his head, you have the mind of Christ.

5. **WATER AND BLOOD:** NEW BIRTH, and the birth of the Church: The blood and water that came out of his side moved us from religion, and tradition to a church.
    a. This was declaring the birth of grace versus the Law.
    b. Water that came out of the side speaks of sanctification.

Day Watches

The blood that came out of his side also speaks of Redemption.

6. Stripes in His body speaks of the 39 major diseases in the world that were defeated at the cross of Calvary. By His stripes we are healed.
7. **Sweat as though it were drops of blood:** sin was transferred into jesus' body before crucifixion. Sin has no hold over your life, and the wages of sin is death, and Jesus paid that price. He became sin that we can be free from its bondage. (The transfer of sin in Jesus' body was so *PAINFUL*, and He was weak, and the Angel came and strengthened him).

- **Internal wound means:**
    a. Injury done to a living tissue by a deep cut or heavy blow.
    b. Pain inflicted on one's feelings.
    c. Injury to one's reputation

"Then released he Barabbas unto them: and when he had scourged Jesus, he delivered him to be crucified" (Matthew 27:26 KJV).

Jesus's internal wound speaks of binding up the broken-hearted.

The broken-hearted are those who are deeply afflicted and distressed on any account

- It may be either on own account of sins,
- Of captivity and oppression by the enemy.
- Death in the family: Loss of relations and friends. The Redeemer came and was wounded that he might apply the balm of consolation, and give us joy and peace.

Watch and Pray

"He healeth the broken in heart, and bindeth up their wounds" (Psalm 147:3 KJV).

- He healeth the broken in heart as a result of divorce, abuse, rejection, accusations and disgrace.
- Every physical injury result in emotional trauma and spiritual trauma that manifests in the form of fear and feelings of rejection.
- Jesus' love and His wounds are still available even today to bind up our wounds. You can hide yourself and the loved ones in His wounds. Amen.

"From the sole of the foot even unto the head there is no soundness in it; but wounds, and bruises, and putrefying sores: they have not been closed, neither bound up, neither mollified with ointment" (Isaiah 1:6 KJV).

THIRD WATCH
THE WATCH OF SHAKING OF FOUNDATIONS & JUDGMENT (12:00 Noon - 3:00 PM)

(See John 4:6; Matt. 27:45; Acts 26:13; Jer. 15:8, Job 11:13-20; Psalm 37:20; Dan. 6:13)

The time for divine guidance and deliverance from evil

Midday watch or the Fullness of Day. (See Psalm 55:17, Proverbs 4:18, Isaiah 58:10, Job 11:15, Psalm 37:3, Jeremiah 20:16).

1. Time to Judge the Arrows and traps of the Enemy against your Life. This hour of prayer is very important to pray against the arrows that fly at noonday. (See Psalm 91:5-6).
1. It is the time to pray and dwell in the secret place of the Most High, abiding under the shadow of the Almighty, and making the Most High your habitation.
2. It is also the time of exercising your God given dominion over Satanic Powers. (See Proverbs 4:18).

The midday is the fullness of the day and it is the beginning of the afternoon.

Watch and Pray

1. Declare the fullness of Joy, life and health. (As the Sun is Full)
2. Let the sun smite your enemies at midday in Jesus Name.
3. Pray against destruction, remember the spirit of destruction is released at midday, and is stalking and persecuting the godly. Pray and refuse to be destructed. Especially in the place of work and business.
4. Declare that justice shall come to you in Jesus name.
5. Declare God's compassion and mercy upon your life.

FOURTH WATCH
HOUR OF PRAYER (15h00-18h00)
TIME TO SEE THE SPIRITUAL VISIONS

This is the hour of prayer

"Who shall ascend into the hill of the LORD? or who shall stand in his holy place?" (Psalm 24:3 KJV).

- Pray for angelic visitation and intervention like in the life of Cornelius and Peter. (See Zechariah 1:10-11, 18-21).
- Receive the finishing anointing as Jesus finished at this hour; whatever you start, you shall finish in Jesus Mighty name.
- Declare that whatever affliction you are going through; it is finished in Jesus Mighty name.
- Declare your salvation and the salvation of your family members as Jesus' death at this hour spoke deliverance from sin and limitations.

(See Luke 23:44-46; Acts 3:1; 10:3, 30-32).

"Now Peter and John went up together into the temple at the hour of prayer, being the ninth hour" (Act 3:1 KJV).

Watch and Pray

"And Cornelius said, Four days ago I was fasting until this hour; and at the ninth hour I prayed in my house, and, behold, a man stood before me in bright clothing" (Act 10:30 KJV).

Time to change history

"When Jesus therefore had received the vinegar, he said, it is finished: and he bowed his head, and gave up the ghost" (John 19:30 KJV).

- The distant past changed, every legal hold of the devil sin, curse and the law was broken at the cross.

Resurrection hour

"And the graves were opened; and many bodies of the saints which slept arose, (Matthew 27:52 KJV).

What the enemy thought he killed and buried came back to life. You are coming out of every grave, and with your wealth, marriage, children and health, and this time to rule and reign with Christ.

The hour of access

"And, behold, the veil of the temple was rent in twain from the top to the bottom; and the earth did quake, and the rocks rent" (Matthew 27:51 KJV).

- This is the clear sign of God's mercy that came from His throne to mankind.
- The veil that concealed the potential of the church from having a fellowship with God was torn; everybody can now have access to the secret place.

Day Watches

The hour of earth quake

- When the Earth quaked, the rock rented and something's resurrected to life.
- Your family's joy, peace, financial breakthrough, ministry and calling is resurrecting to life.

The hour of darkness and turning point

- Jesus was in agony fighting against the powers of darkness.
- He was made to be sin, who never knew sin.
- His soul was made a sin offering.
- He was separated from the Father; He invaded hell to get the keys of death for us, and He led a procession of many who died and were waiting for the promise of paradise.
- The mission of salvation was accomplished at this hour as He led the procession out of Hades to paradise.
- Jesus uttered Psalm 22:1- He allowed Himself to be separated from the Father and be sin so He could gain us.

The hour of triumph

Just before Christ died, he spoke in his full strength, to show that his life was not forced from him, but was freely delivered into his Father's hands. He had strength to bid defiance to the powers of death: and to show that by the eternal Spirit He offered Himself, being the Priest as well as the

Watch and Pray

Sacrifice, He cried with a loud voice. Then He yielded up the ghost.

This is the time of the evening sacrifice. It was at this time that Elijah called forth fire from Heaven to consume the prophets of Baal on Mount Carmel (See 1 Kings 18:29, 30, 36-39, Isaiah 17:12-14, Matthew 27:45-61, Luke 27:45-47, Daniel 3:25, 9:21, Genesis 24:63, Acts 3:1, 10:1-32, Zechariah 6:1, Revelations 6:1).

The time to Shape History

This was the time where God turned his back on sin to usher in a new era. For the new day to come, night should come first. That is why darkness covered the whole earth. That marked the ushering of a new era for the earth and mankind. "Behold I made everything new."

- Celebration in hell that brought a surprise visitation. A visitation of Victory to the earth and its inhabitants specifically those who believe.
- If they knew who He was, they would have not crucified the Lord of Glory.
- Satan himself thought he knew who God and the Word were. Only to discover that he will be beaten and stripped off in his own territory.
- When Jesus gave up the ghost, history was changed forever, because He now cut a covenant for us with God, and there was a triumphant Glory over hell, death and the grave.
- At that hour, darkness departed. The covering of darkness cast over the nations is broken, just enforce it.

Day Watches

- A new generation was birthed. A generation that will be turned away from sin and serve with power. He said "Eloi, Eloi, Lama Sabachthani" meaning "My God, my God, why have you forsaken me?"

It is time to forsake every weight that pulls us down from worshipping God freely. You are called with a High Calling. Let the earth quake and open its mouth and swallow every enemy pursuing your life, family and ministry.

Watch and Pray

CHAPTER TWENTY

POWER OF THE HOLY COMMUNION

HOW CAN I USE THE HOLY COMMUNION IN SPIRITUAL WARFARE?

JESUS said, just before instituting the Lord's supper, *"With desire have I desired to eat this Passover with you before I suffer" (Matthew 22:15).* This is a Hebrew manner of expression, signifying *"I have greatly desired."* He had desired it, doubtless:

1. That He might institute the Lord's Supper, to be a perpetual memorial of Him;
2. That He might strengthen them for their approaching trials;
3. That He might explain to them the true nature of the Passover; and;
4. That He might spend another season with them in the duties of religion and faith.

The Holy Communion

- Jesus took the bread - That is, the unleavened bread which they used at the celebration of the Passover, made into thin cakes, easily broken and distributed.

Watch and Pray

- And blessed it - "gave thanks" to God for it.
- And broke it - This "breaking" of the bread represented the sufferings of Jesus that was about to take place - His body wounded for sin. 1 Corinthians 11:24 adds, *"This is my body which is broken for you,"* that is, which is about to be broken for you by death, or wounded, pierced, bruised, to make atonement for your sins.
- He gave to His disciples to partake.

The origin of the Blood (See Matthew 26:27)

When God created man in His own image, He breathed into his nostrils the breath of life, and man became a living soul. In simple terms, we can say the collision of the body of a man and the breath of God caused life (blood), and the life of any living being is in the blood.

- *"For the life of the flesh is in the blood: and I have given it to you upon the altar to make an atonement for your souls: for it is the blood that maketh an atonement for the soul"* (Leviticus 17:11 KJV).
- Blood is the precious gift from God to mankind that is why after the fall in Eden it required the blood to cover man's sins. When Adam and Eve sinned, it was necessary for God to slaughter an innocent animal to cover them. It was not about the skin of an animal only, but also the shedding of the Innocent Blood.
- *"... and without shedding of blood is no remission of sins"* (Hebrews 9:22b KJV).
- The breath of God on Adam's body created blood, and Adam became a living soul. The very same

breath of God's spirit was breathed into Mary's womb, and Jesus was conceived. Adam carried the DNA of God and Jesus as well carried the DNA of God, not that of Joseph.

How to use the blood of Jesus in prayer?

- Use the blood of the lamb of god as a hedge of protection and a *sign* of His presence in your life, home, office and Ministry.
    - It dates back to Egypt: the blood was a sign that they have a covenant with God.
    - The applied blood of the slaughtered Lamb spoke protection and preservation from the Angel of death.
    - The absence of the blood was a sign of where to kill.
- (See Matthew 26:27). And when He had taken a cup and given thanks, He gave it to them, saying, 'Drink from it, all of you; for this is My blood of the new and better covenant, which is being poured out for many for the forgiveness of sins.
- This cup is the New Testament in my blood. (See Matthew 26:26, 28).
- Jesus' blood represents "His life" (See Genesis 9:4; Leviticus 17:14).
- It was forbidden, therefore, to eat blood of the animal, because it contained its life. Therefore, Jesus says that His blood was shed for many, it is the same as saying that His life was given for many. When we drink His

Watch and Pray

blood we receive His life and therefore, becomes one with Him.
- The blood of the lamb spoke mercy and preservation in Egypt upon the Israel.
- All nourishment for the body comes through blood. And diseases as well can be traced through blood testing.
- (See Romans 3:25; Matthew 26:29-30).
- And when they had sung a hymn - The Passover was observed by the Jews by singing Psalm 113–118.

"And being in an agony He prayed more earnestly: and his sweat was as it were great drops of blood falling down to the ground" (Luke 22:44 KJV).

As you engage in spiritual warfare for your family, health, and business, you can prepare the communion meal. Sing hymns to the Lord, repent and acknowledge your sins of commission and omission. Give thanks to the Lord and bless the communion meal.

Begin to declare what you are trusting God for, as you partake and remember the finished work of the cross.

In conclusion

Believers partake of the communion for the following reason:

- We do this act in remembrance of the Lord, this is one of the instructions the Lord gave to His disciples, the church
- To remind the devil of His defeat at the Cross and His future.

Day Watches

- To eat more of His body and His Blood so He can increase and everything else diminish, and we experience and receive health and healing.
- To enter into a covenant with the Lord and seal Godly covenants

We do this act to celebrate the life of Christ and declare His second coming.

Watch and Pray

CHAPTER TWENTYONE

HOW TO DEAL WITH ACCUSATIONS OF THE ENEMY IN THE WORKPLACE AND IN BUSINESS

The enemy uses human vessels to assassinate the character of the righteous with the intent to exterminate their destinies. The righteous must see beyond the intention and expectation of the enemy and retaliate against the devises of the enemy. Praise the Lord for His word which is relevant yesterday, today, and forever. Psalm 109 is an intercessory prayer that confronts and deals with the enemy. The enemy will not escape the sword of this psalm, and the destiny assassin will be assassinated and his name will be erased from under the sun.

Confess with me this Psalm of judgement upon the enemies of your life and progress in Jesus Mighty Name.

"Hold not thy peace, O God of my praise; For the mouth of the wicked and the mouth of deceit have they opened against me: They have spoken unto me with a lying tongue. They have compassed me about also with words of hatred, and fought against me without a cause. For my love they are my adversaries: But I give myself unto prayer. And they have rewarded me evil for good, and hatred for my love" (Psalm 109:1-5 KJV).

Watch and Pray

- **Solution to Dealing with the Enemy in your Life, Work and Home.**

"Set thou a wicked man over him; And let an adversary stand at his right hand. When he is judged, let him come forth guilty; And let his prayer be turned into sin. Let his days be few; And let another take his office. Let his children be fatherless, And his wife a widow. Let his children be vagabonds, and beg; And let them seek their bread out of their desolate places. Let the extortioner catch all that he hath; And let strangers make spoil of his labour. there be none to extend kindness unto him; Neither let there be any to have pity on his fatherless children. Let his posterity be cut off; In the generation following let their name be blotted out. Let the iniquity of his fathers be remembered with Jehovah; And let not the sin of his mother be blotted out. Let them be before Jehovah continually, that he may cut off the memory of them from the earth; Because he remembered not to show kindness, but persecuted the poor and needy man, And the broken in heart, to slay them. Yea, he loved cursing, and it came unto him; And he delighted not in blessing, and it was far from him. He clothed himself also with cursing as with his garment, and it came into his inward parts like water, And like oil into his bones. Let it be unto him as the raiment wherewith he covereth himself, and for the girdle wherewith he is girded continually. This is the reward of mine adversaries from Jehovah, and of them that speak evil against my soul" (Psalm 109:6-20 KJV).

Prayer of personal intercession

"But deal thou with me, O Jehovah the Lord, for thy name's sake: Because thy loving-kindness is good, deliver thou me; For I am poor and needy, and my heart is wounded within me. I am gone like the shadow when it declineth: I am tossed up and down as the locust. My knees are weak through fasting; And my flesh faileth of fatness. I am become also a reproach unto them: When they see me, they shake their head. Help me,

How to Deal with Accusations by the Enemy in the Place of Work and Business

O Jehovah my God; Oh save me according to thy lovingkindness: they may know that this is thy hand; That thou, Jehovah, hast done it. Let them curse, but bless thou: When they arise, they shall be put to shame, but thy servant shall rejoice. Let mine adversaries be clothed with dishonor, and let them cover themselves with their own shame as with a robe" (Psalm 109:21-29 KJV).

Prayer of thanksgiving for victory

"I will give great thanks unto Jehovah with my mouth; Yea, I will praise Him among the multitude. For He will stand at the right hand of the needy, to save Him from them that judge his soul" (Psalm 109:30-31 KJV).

Conclusion remarks

Be strong in the Lord and in the Power of His Mighty...

Watch and Pray

References

Branden, G., 2005. God Code. In: *God Code.* s.l.:s.n., pp. 122,137,138.

ABOUT THE AUTHOR

Pastor Portia Mange is an apostolic and prophetic revolutionary labouring to see a global revival both in the church and at the marketplace. She is raised by God to divinely teach and raise prayer warriors, intercessors and watchmen who will possess the power and authority to influence individuals, institutions and governments back to God.

STAY CONNECTED WITH PASTOR PORTIA

Email: pstportia@yahoo.co.uk

Tel: +27 82 088 8517

Social Media: Facebook.com/PstPortiaMange

www.ingramcontent.com/pod-product-compliance
Lightning Source LLC
LaVergne TN
LVHW091109080426
835510LV00033B/175